# DANGEROUS
# DECREES
## *That* DESTROY STRONGHOLDS

D1522594

# DANGEROUS DECREES

## *That* DESTROY STRONGHOLDS

*Powerful Prayers That Arrest Demons &*
*Crush Satan's Strategies Against Your Life*

## DR. FRANCIS MYLES

DESTINY IMAGE® PUBLISHERS, INC.

P.O. Box 310, Shippensburg, PA 17257-0310

*"Publishing cutting-edge prophetic resources to supernaturally empower the body of Christ"*

This book and all other Destiny Image and Destiny Image Fiction books are available at Christian bookstores and distributors worldwide.

For more information on foreign distributors, call 717-532-3040.

Reach us on the Internet: www.destinyimage.com.

ISBN 13 TP: 978-0-7684-7677-4

ISBN 13 eBook: 978-0-7684-7678-1

For Worldwide Distribution, Printed in the U.S.A.

1 2 3 4 5 6 7 8 / 28 27 26 25 24

# Contents

# PART ONE

## *Dangerous Decrees*

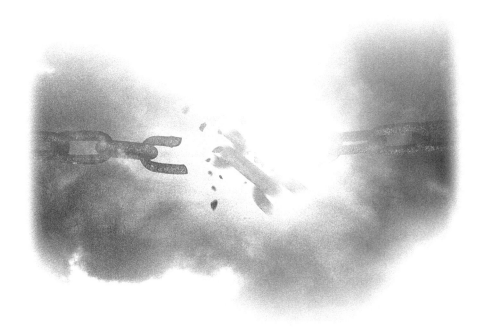

# Preface

You will also decree a thing, and it will be established for you; and light will shine on your ways (**Job 22:28 NASB1995**).

Finally, a book on the "power of dangerous decrees" that will help you destroy strongholds in your life. The concept of dangerous decrees from the courts of Heaven in this writing refers to the authoritative pronouncements that originate from the throne of God, which have the power to dismantle spiritual strongholds in the life of every follower of Christ. These decrees, as reflected in the Scriptures, are not dangerous in the sense of causing harm to those who are righteous but are dangerous to the forces of darkness.

In Job 22:28, the power of a righteous decree is clearly evident. When spoken in alignment with God's will, such apostolic and prophetic decrees have the power to effect change and bring about God's intended will and purpose. These apostolic and prophetic decrees can break the strongholds of despair and hopelessness, while simultaneously dispelling spiritual darkness by the light of God.

Deuteronomy 4:40 shows us a decree of obedience that carries a promise of well-being and longevity for those who adhere to its tenets. It contains a divine mandate that, when followed, has the power to destroy the strongholds of lawlessness and rebellion in the life of believers. This particular decree upholds the order of God's creation and the blessings inherent in living according to the laws of the Kingdom.

This life-changing book, *Dangerous Decrees That Destroy Strongholds* is intended to introduce the body of Christ to the awesome power of the realm of "decrees." Decrees for the most part fall under the realm of kingship! Kings make decrees, which immediately gives them the force of law! For instance, in Daniel 6:26 (NKJV), King Darius declares, *"I make a decree that in all the dominion of my kingdom men must tremble and fear before the God of Daniel; for He is the living God, and steadfast forever; His kingdom is one which shall not be destroyed, and His dominion shall endure to the end."*

The decree issued by King Darius in Daniel 6:26, after witnessing Daniel's miraculous survival in the lions' den, acknowledges the sovereignty of God. This royal decree was dangerous to the spiritual strongholds of idolatry and human arrogance, as it directed all to revere the true and living God, whose dominion is everlasting. Those who dared to challenge the decree met with sudden death.

In Jonah 3:7 (NIV), we are confronted with the decree of repentance issued by another king to avoid national judgment: *"This is the proclamation he issued in Nineveh: 'By the decree of the king and his nobles: Do not let people or animals, herds or flocks, taste anything; do not let them eat or drink.'"* The king of Nineveh's decree for fasting and repentance demonstrates the power of a decree to break the strongholds of wickedness and impending judgment over an entire country. This is a lesson from history for all world leaders. It shows that a king's or presidential decree that is divinely inspired can lead to national transformation and deliverance from total destruction.

In Jeremiah 5:22 (NASB), God Himself declares, *"'Do you not fear Me?' declares the Lord. 'Do you not tremble in My presence? For I have placed the sand as a boundary for the sea, an eternal limit, and it will not cross over it. Though the waves toss, they cannot prevail; though they roar, they will not cross over it.'"* God speaks of a decree that He has issued that sets the boundaries for the seas (oceans), which is also a metaphor for the limits He places on human chaos and destruction. This divine decree is dangerous to the strongholds of chaos and disorder, illustrating that God's decrees bring stability and order to both the natural and spiritual worlds.

*Dangerous Decrees That Destroy Strongholds* is a book you will find loaded with apostolic and prophetic decrees that will radically change your life. Each of these decrees carries the weight of God's government, and when pronounced in faith, they will enact God's will in your life as it is in Heaven. These decrees will help you bring deliverance and establish divine order in the face of spiritual opposition. The many Scriptures used in this book collectively affirm the transformative power of heavenly decrees to destroy the fortresses of evil and usher in the rule of God's Kingdom.

Yours for His Kingdom,
**Dr. Francis Myles**
Author, *The Order of Melchizedek*

# CHAPTER 1

# You Shall Decree a Thing!

You will also decree a thing, and it will be established for you; and light will shine on your ways (**Job 22:28 NASB1995**).

I n the realm of spiritual warfare and biblical anthropology, the concept of making decrees holds a significant place within the economy of glory. The practice of "making decrees" unfortunately is often misunderstood or overlooked by so many citizens of the Kingdom of God. Unfortunately for them, the practice of making decrees is deeply rooted in Scripture and carries profound spiritual implications for the life of a believer.

This book, *Dangerous Decrees That Destroy Strongholds,* aims to explore the biblical basis for making decrees, focusing on key Scriptures such as Job 22:28, and to demonstrate why this apostolic and prophetic technology is vitally important in the life of any follower of Christ who desires to become an overcomer. I don't know about you, but defeat is no longer part of my spiritual vocabulary because I am fully persuaded of my victory over demonic entities because of the perfect and finished work of Yeshua the Messiah on the Cross.

## Understanding Biblical Decrees

> *Moreover Issue a decree as to what you shall do for the elders*
> *of these Jews, for the building of this house of God: Let the cost*
> *be paid at the king's expense from taxes on the region beyond*
> *the River; this is to be given immediately to these men, so that*
> *they are not hindered* (Ezra 6:8 NKJV).

To fully grasp the apostolic concept of decrees in a biblical sense, it's essential to understand what a decree really is within the economy of glory. In the Bible, a *decree is a declaration made with authority*, this decree is often rooted in the divine will of God. In some cases, the decree is tied to a person's position in government. A decree is more than just wishful speaking or thinking; it's a supernatural statement of faith that aligns with God's promises and purposes.

Job 22:28 (NASB1995) declares, *"You will also decree a thing, and it will be established for you; and light will shine on your ways."* In my humble opinion, this verse from the book of Job is one of the most important Scriptures on the subject of "decrees." The passage from Job emphasizes the power of a righteous person's decree. When God's children are perfectly aligned with His will, such prophetic declarations have the power to bring about radical change and manifest God's promises in the physical realm.

Based upon Job 22:28, there are three key components to a biblical decree, namely:

1.  The "thing" that is being spoken into existence! This means that before making a decree we must know "the thing" that we want to decree and why. This first step helps us maintain spiritual harmony with the will of God as revealed in the Bible. For instance we cannot decree the death of our enemies who Christ died for, simply because they made us uncomfortable in the flesh.

2. The second critical component of a biblically sound apostolic and prophetic decree is incorporated in the expression, *it will be established for you;* meaning that God is the real power behind the manifestation of a prophetic decree. God is One who works in the invisible world of the spirit to bring to pass the "thing" which is being decreed.

3. The third and final component of a biblical prophetic and apostolic decree is the "superior energy of the Light," which is released after a decree has been made to overthrow the reign of "darkness" and its many insidious agents that are opposed to the manifestation of the "thing" we are decreeing. I am reminded of John 1:5 (NASB1995) that says, *"And the light shines in the darkness, and the darkness did not comprehend it."* When we make an apostolic and prophetic decree in all boldness, we unleash the Light of God with all its superior elements of dominion over the darkness.

## The Cyrus Decree: A Major Turning Point

*Now in the first year of Cyrus king of Persia, that the word of the Lord by the mouth of Jeremiah might be fulfilled, the Lord stirred up the spirit of Cyrus king of Persia, so that he made a proclamation throughout all his kingdom, and also put it in writing, saying, Thus says Cyrus king of Persia: All the kingdoms of the earth the Lord God of heaven has given me. And He has commanded me to build Him a house at Jerusalem which is in Judah. Who is among you of all His people? May his God be with him, and let him go up to Jerusalem which is in Judah, and build the house of the Lord God of Israel (He is God), which is in Jerusalem. And whoever is left in any place where he dwells, let the men of his place help him with silver and gold, with goods and livestock, besides the freewill offerings for the house of God which is in Jerusalem* (Ezra 1:1-4 NKJV).

In Ezra 1:1-4, King Cyrus makes an unusual decree that would forever change the course of history for Jews in exile, long displaced from the homeland God gave to their fathers, Abraham, Isaac, and Jacob. King Cyrus's decree represented a monumental shift for the Jewish exiles. After decades of captivity in Babylon, the Cyrus decree provided a formal authorization for the Jewish people to return to Jerusalem and rebuild their fallen temple. The prayers of the prophet of Daniel in Babylon and the prophecy of Jeremiah had just been fulfilled. The decree of Cyrus was not only a political and social turning point, it was also a spiritual reawakening, a revival so to speak for the exiled Jewish community and the remnant who remained in Jerusalem during the 70 years of captivity.

## Critical Components of the Cyrus Decree

The decree made by King Cyrus to destroy any demonic, economic, social, and political strongholds that were standing in the "way" of the fulfillment of the Word of the Lord through the prophet Jeremiah consisted of several critical components. Namely:

### Economic and Material Support

The decree wasn't merely permissive; it included provisions for financial and material support for the rebuilding efforts of the temple in Jerusalem. This aspect of the decree was crucial, as it provided the practical means for the exiles to reconstruct the temple, a task that would have been financially overwhelming for a people just emerging from captivity. This part of the Cyrus decree is proof that Cyrus, a Gentile king, was divinely inspired by Yahweh to make the decree. God never calls us to do something significant in His Kingdom and not supernaturally provide the resources needed for us to fully obey Him!

## Legitimization and Protection

King Cyrus's proclamation provided a measure of legitimacy to the Jewish returnees in the eyes of surrounding peoples, regional and national governments under the control or influence of Cyrus. Cyrus's decree acted as a protective edict, "a restraining order" so to speak, ensuring that local governors and officials assisted the Jews rather than hinder them. This protection was essential for the success of the rebuilding project and for the safety of the returnees. This is even more critical when you consider that many of Cyrus's own subjects and nobles despised the Jews and saw them merely as slaves in captivity.

## Religious and Cultural Implications

The rebuilding of the temple in Jerusalem went beyond physical reconstruction. We know from Scripture that the natural is simply the fruit of spiritual forces or technologies imposing their will on the natural order of things. Cyrus's decree symbolized the spiritual restoration of Jewish religious practices and cultural identity. The decree, thus, had profound religious and cultural implications, as it facilitated the reestablishment of worship according to the Torah, which helped to solidify Jewish identity post-exile. What a God we serve!

## Sociopolitical Impact

By allowing the Jewish people to return and rebuild the temple in Jerusalem, King Cyrus's decree effectively recognized the rights of the Jewish people to self-determination in their ancestral homeland. This set a precedent for the concept of a nation's right to exist and govern itself according to its cultural and religious precepts. Most importantly, the Cyrus decree, recorded in the ancient scrolls of Babylon and acknowledged by most historians, acts as irrefutable proof that the Jewish people are the rightful owners of their ancestral land of Israel, politically referred to as Palestine, even though the so-called Palestinians have only existed in that part of the world for less than 500 years; whereas the Jewish people have been there for at least 3,000 years.

## Fulfillment of Prophecy

For the Jewish people, Cyrus's decree was seen as the fulfillment of God's promise to end the Babylonian captivity after 70 years of captivity, as prophesied by Jeremiah. It reinforced their faith in God's sovereignty and His faithfulness to His covenant and promise He made to Abraham. This deeply impacted their spiritual outlook on life and strengthened their spiritual bond to the God of Abraham, Isaac, and Jacob. It also helped them believe in their own manifest destiny as a people.

## Long-Term Consequences of the Cyrus Decree

The long-term impact of the decree of King Cyrus is truly immeasurable. The decree set in motion prophetic events that would shape Jewish history forever. The second temple, which arose from the decree, stood for several centuries and became the focal point of Jewish worship until its destruction in 70 AD, after the Romans invaded Jerusalem. The return from exile and the rebuilding of the temple are commemorated annually in the Jewish festival of Passover, serving as lasting reminders of Jewish perseverance and divine providence. King Cyrus's decree in Ezra 6:8 was a cornerstone event that helped to reshape the destiny of the Jewish people, facilitating their return from exile, the rebuilding of the temple, and the reestablishment of their religious and cultural life. It also stands as a lasting testament to the convergence of divine prophecy and human agency in the historical and spiritual restoration of the Jewish people to their covenanted homeland of Israel.

## Biblical Examples of Decrees

*Then God said, "Let there be light"; and there was light* (Genesis 1:3 NKJV).

*Then He arose and rebuked the wind, and said to the sea, "Peace, be still!" And the wind ceased and there was a great calm* (Mark 4:39 NKJV).

*When Jesus saw their faith, He said to the paralytic, "Son, your sins are forgiven you"* (Mark 2:5 NKJV).

Throughout the Bible and in studying the economy of glory, there are numerous instances where decrees played a pivotal role in the manifestation of what the Lord required. For instance, in the creation narrative, God's decrees brought this amazingly intricate universe into existence when God decreed, *"Let there be light,"* (Genesis 1:3). Similarly, Yeshua's (Jesus) ministry is marked by authoritative declarations such as calming the storm (Mark 4:39) and declaring the forgiveness of sins (Mark 2:5).

In Acts chapters 5 and 13, we see two very powerful instances when an apostolic decree was issued that drastically changed the spiritual landscape. In Acts 5, the apostle Peter issued a decree, which resulted in the immediate deaths of Ananias and Saphira, a Jewish couple in the church at Jerusalem who connived to deceive the Holy Spirit concerning the actual price they had sold their land for. The Scriptures capture the incident this way:

> But a certain man named Ananias, with Sapphira his wife, sold a possession. And he kept back part of the proceeds, his wife also being aware of it, and brought a certain part and laid it at the apostles' feet. But Peter said, "Ananias, why has Satan filled your heart to lie to the Holy Spirit and keep back part of the price of the land for yourself? While it remained, was it not your own? And after it was sold, was it not in your own control? Why have you conceived this thing in your heart? You have not lied to men but to God." Then Ananias, hearing these words, fell down and breathed his last. So great fear came upon all those who heard these things. And the young men arose and wrapped him up, carried him out, and buried him. Now it was about three hours later when his wife came in, not knowing what had happened. And Peter answered her, "Tell me whether you sold the land for so much?" She said, "Yes, for so much." Then Peter said to her, "How is it that you have agreed together to test the Spirit of the Lord? Look, the feet of those who have buried your husband are at the door, and they will carry you out." Then immediately she fell down at his feet and breathed her last. And the young men came in and found her dead, and carrying her out, buried her by her husband (Acts 5:1-10 NKJV).

Peter's apostolic decree that led to the deaths of Ananias and his wife brought the fear of the Lord to bear upon the entire church in Jerusalem. Everyone who heard the story realized that the Holy Spirit is not a child's toy you can play with. He is an equal member of the eternal Godhead worthy of all our reverence, fear, and adoration.

Peter's decree was followed by another equally important decree made in Acts 13 by the apostle Paul. The Bible records this apostolic decree this way:

> *Now when they had gone through the island to Paphos, they found a certain sorcerer, a false prophet, a Jew whose name was Bar-Jesus, who was with the proconsul, Sergius Paulus, an intelligent man. This man called for Barnabas and Saul and sought to hear the word of God. But Elymas the sorcerer (for so his name is translated) withstood them, seeking to turn the proconsul away from the faith. Then Saul, who also is called Paul, filled with the Holy Spirit, looked intently at him and said, "O full of all deceit and all fraud, you son of the devil, you enemy of all righteousness, will you not cease perverting the straight ways of the Lord? And now, indeed, the hand of the Lord is upon you, and you shall be blind, not seeing the sun for a time." And immediately a dark mist fell on him, and he went around seeking someone to lead him by the hand. Then the proconsul believed, when he saw what had been done, being astonished at the teaching of the Lord* (Acts 13:6-12 NKJV).

Wow! I would have paid anything to be in the front-row seat to observe first the power of this apostolic decree. This false prophet, Bar-Jesus, was nothing but a sorcerer masquerading as a prophet of God. He made the unfortunate mistake of coming up against one of God's apostolic generals, Paul, when he was sent to preach the gospel to the city's governor. Paul made a decree that this sorcerer's eyes would go "blind for a season" before he saw again! The decree happened to him, immediately. The power of this decree shocked the proconsul Sergius Paulus so much, he quickly gave his life to Christ! Are you ready to add your decrees to the biblical canon of decrees that have been made by holy men and women as they were moved by the Holy Spirit?

## The Authority Behind Decrees!

This juncture of our unfolding revelation brings us into a critical question: "Where does the authority to make decrees come from?" The answer is simple but deeply profound. The believer's authority to make biblical decrees (decrees according to the will of God) stems from the believer's relationship with God through the Person and finished work of Yeshua (Jesus). As children of God, believers are granted the authority to speak and act in alignment with God's will. This authority is not based on human soulish power but on the believer's abiding faith in God and anchored in a deep understanding of His Word, the Bible. The tenets and scope of the believer's authority in Christ are well tabulated in the following passages of Scriptures. Please meditate on them daily, until they are fully memorized into a spiritual consciousness of eternal awareness!

> *Behold, I give you the authority to trample on serpents and scorpions, and over all the power of the enemy, and nothing shall by any means hurt you* (Luke 10:19 NKJV).

> *And He said to them, "Go into all the world and preach the gospel to every creature. He who believes and is baptized will be saved; but he who does not believe will be condemned. And these signs will follow those who believe: In My name they will cast out demons; they will speak with new tongues; they will take up serpents; and if they drink anything deadly, it will by no means hurt them; they will lay hands on the sick, and they will recover"* (Mark 16:15-18 NKJV).

## The Purpose and Power of Decrees

Before we conclude our chapter on "You Shall Decree a Thing!" we need to understand the purpose and power of decrees. Decrees serve multiple spiritual purposes in the life of a Christ-following believer, namely:

1. **Faith Activation:** Decrees are a supernatural way to actively express faith, by speaking God's promises into existence. Nothing activates faith quicker than the spoken word, expressed in a spirit of boldness. *"Now, Lord, look on their threats, and grant to Your servants that with all boldness they may speak Your word, by stretching out Your hand to heal, and that signs and wonders may be done through the name of Your holy Servant Jesus." And when they had prayed, the place where they were assembled together was shaken; and they were all filled with the Holy Spirit, and they spoke the word of God with boldness"* (Acts 4:29-31 NKJV).

2. **Spiritual Warfare:** In the context of spiritual warfare, decrees are a tool for asserting God's truth and power over the lies and schemes of the enemy. Decrees allow us to paraphrase the revealed will of God as tabulated by Scripture and formulate it (the will of God) into words of command that allow us to ignite our faith and activate our God-given spiritual authority to destroy demonic strongholds. *"For the weapons of our warfare are not carnal but mighty in God for pulling down strongholds, casting down arguments and every high thing that exalts itself against the knowledge of God, bringing every thought into captivity to the obedience of Christ"* (2 Corinthians 10:4-5 NKJV).

3. **Alignment with God's Will:** Decrees help align the believer's thoughts and actions with God's will, leading to a more purposeful and directed Kingdom lifestyle. Since decrees allow us to paraphrase the truth of Scripture into summarized prayer

points and commands, they act as catalysts for helping us stay aligned with the will of God. *"You will also declare a thing, and it will be established for you; so light will shine on your ways"* (Job 22:28 NKJV).

## Practical Application: Making Biblical Decrees

I am a man who believes that you cannot help people manifest the supernatural power of God, unless you can show them how to practically "apply the spiritual truths" they have been taught. In keeping faith with my ministerial philosophy, I want to state that making biblical, apostolic, and prophetic decrees involves several key steps:

### Scriptural Foundation

Decrees should be grounded in Scripture, reflecting God's promises and character. God will never get behind a decree no matter who makes it, which contradicts both Scripture and the revealed character of God. For instance, decreeing that a married man you have a romantic crush for will divorce his wife and marry you, is a demonically inspired and soulish decree, rooted in the worst case of charismatic witchcraft that one can imagine. How can the God of Scripture honor such a decree? He won't! *"Your word I have hidden in my heart, that I might not sin against You. Blessed are You, O Lord! Teach me Your statutes. With my lips I have declared all the judgments of Your mouth"* (Psalm 119:11-13 NKJV).

### Faith and Conviction

Believers should make decrees with faith and conviction, believing in the power of God to bring them to fruition. Faith requires the spoken word to mobilize itself into positive action. *"(as it is written, 'I have made you a father of many nations') in the presence of Him whom he believed—God, who gives life to the dead and calls those things which do not exist as though they did; who, contrary to hope, in hope believed, so that he became the father of many nations, according to what was spoken, 'So shall your descendants be'"* (Romans 4:17-18 NKJV).

## Alignment with God's Will

It's crucial that decrees are made in alignment with God's will and purpose, not personal and soulish desires. Yeshua, in the Garden of Gethsemane, beautifully demonstrated this truth to us in the hour of His passion as He interceded for the "cup of suffering" that was descending on Him to pass away. With the awesome power Yeshua had as the perfect and incarnate Son of God, He could have easily decreed away this cup of suffering! However, as soon as He realized in prayer that the cup of suffering was the will of His heavenly Father, Jesus quickly yielded His personal will to the will of God. *"When He came to the place, He said to them, 'Pray that you may not enter into temptation.' And He was withdrawn from them about a stone's throw, and He knelt down and prayed, saying, 'Father, if it is Your will, take this cup away from Me; nevertheless not My will, but Yours, be done.' Then an angel appeared to Him from heaven, strengthening Him. And being in agony, He prayed more earnestly. Then His sweat became like great drops of blood falling down to the ground"* (Luke 22:40-44 NKJV).

In closing, the practice of making biblically accurate apostolic and prophetic decrees is a powerful aspect of Kingdom living. Rooted in the truth of Scripture and empowered by our faith, these prophetic declarations are a means by which believers can activate their faith and God-given authority to engage in spiritual warfare, while simultaneously aligning ourselves more closely with God's will. As exemplified by Job 22:28, which has been our anchor Scripture in addition to other Scriptures, the act of decreeing is not only a biblical mandate but a vital spiritual tool in the spiritual arsenal of every believer.

In Part Two of this book titled "The Book of Dangerous Decrees and Activation Prayers," I have written some very powerful, biblically sound apostolic and prophetic decrees for your everyday use or as your situation demands.

# Life Application

## *Memory Verse*

> *Moreover I issue a decree as to what you shall do for the elders of these Jews, for the building of this house of God: Let the cost be paid at the king's expense from taxes on the region beyond the River; this is to be given immediately to these men, so that they are not hindered* (Ezra 6:8 NKJV).

## *Reflections*

1. Who does a decree involve?

   Christ following believer

2. How did the decree of King Cyrus affect the Jewish people?

   That would forever change the course of history.

CHAPTER 2

# The Anatomy
# of a Dangerous Prayer

Therefore, confess your sins to one another [your false steps, your offenses], and pray for one another, that you may be healed and restored. The heartfelt and persistent prayer of a righteous man (believer) can accomplish much [when put into action and made effective by God—it is dynamic and can have tremendous power]. Elijah was a man with a nature like ours [with the same physical, mental, and spiritual limitations and shortcomings], and he prayed intensely for it not to rain, and it did not rain on the earth for three years and six months (**James 5:16-17 AMP**).

In the realm of spiritual warfare and deep religious understanding, prayer stands as a pivotal tool, both for maintaining and manifesting true spiritual power with God. *Dangerous prayers, in my humble definition, are biblically sound prayers that are most aligned with God's will and contain certain key elements that foster a profound connection with the eternal Godhead.* These prayers are categorized in the "dangerous" category because they are so biblically sound and contain critical components that inspire instant divine intervention in human affairs. This chapter explores seven biblical references that demonstrate seven critical components, showcasing the eternal importance, power, and immutability of prayer.

## The Anatomy of a Dangerous Prayer: Key Components of Effectiveness

The first critical component of a dangerous prayer is:

### 1. Sincerity and Humility – 2 Chronicles 7:14 (NIV)

> *If my people, who are called by my name, will humble themselves and pray and seek my face and turn from their wicked ways, then I will hear from heaven, and I will forgive their sin and will heal their land.*

Second Chronicles 7:14 (NIV) clearly underscores the importance of humility and sincerity when we are approaching our holy God in prayer. From time immemorial God has always responded positively to prayers that come from a place of genuine repentance and self-awareness. The act of seeking God's face, in the context of 2 Chronicles 7:14, suggests a perpetual striving for a deeper and more intimate relationship with the eternal Godhead, while acknowledging one's own limitations, idiocrasies, and the desperate need for divine guidance that all humans need. The prayers I have written for you in Part Two, "The Book of Dangerous Decree and Activation Prayers," follow the proven pattern laid out in this chapter. Entering the place of prayer filled with a spirit of pride is a proven recipe for disaster. Scripture is already clear on this matter (James 4:6)—God resists the proud and gives grace to those who humble themselves before Him!

The second critical component of a dangerous prayer is:

### 2. Faith and Trust – Mark 11:24 (NIV)

> *Therefore I tell you, whatever you ask for in prayer, believe that you have received it, and it will be yours.*

In Mark 11:24, Yeshua clearly emphasizes the power of faith in prayer. The assurance that what is asked for in prayer, with genuine faith, will be granted by our God, who answers prayer and does not lie, is a cornerstone of effective and fervent prayer. However, faith is not mere wishful thinking or a positive mental attitude, faith is a profound trust in God's omnipotence and benevolence to honor His Word and promises. The writer of Hebrews in the "faith-hall-of-fame" chapter of the Bible, declares, *"But without faith it is impossible to [walk with God and] please Him, for whoever comes [near] to God must [necessarily] believe that God exists and that He rewards those who [earnestly and diligently] seek Him"* (Hebrews 11:6 AMP). So, no one who is weak in faith can pray dangerous prayers! Thankfully, the Scriptures declare that faith comes by hearing and hearing by the Word of God. The Word of God is the Source of mountain-moving faith.

The third critical component of a dangerous prayer is:

## 3. Alignment with God's Will – 1 John 5:14-15 (NIV)

> *This is the confidence we have in approaching God: that if we ask anything according to his will, he hears us. And if we know that he hears us—whatever we ask—we know that we have what we asked of him.*

This passage in 1 John 5 emphasizes the importance of aligning our prayers with God's will. Life this side of Heaven is not just about what we desire, but about seeking what God desires for us. This divine alignment of our will to the will of God ensures that our prayers are not only heard but answered in the way that furthers our spiritual growth and God's plan for mankind. We must never forget that there is no such thing in the Kingdom of God as a personal decision. Every decision we make impacts the Kingdom of God, our destiny, and those who are called to be our destiny helpers. When the prophet Jonah attempted to do his will and ran to Tarshish instead of going to Nineveh as the Lord commanded him, he brought great calamity on a ship filled with innocents who were headed to Tarshish.

The people on the ship and the owner of the ship suffered serious financial losses due to Jonah's disobedience in choosing his will over the revealed will of God. The storm beating down on the ship headed for Tarshish ceased immediately after they threw Jonah overboard where a great whale was waiting to accommodate the disobedient prophet. *"Then they said to him, 'What shall we do to you that the sea may be calm for us?'—for the sea was growing more tempestuous. And he said to them, 'Pick me up and throw me into the sea; then the sea will become calm for you. For I know that this great tempest is because of me.' Nevertheless the men rowed hard to return to land, but they could not, for the sea continued to grow more tempestuous against them"* (Jonah 1:11-13 NKJV). The moral of this story is simply this—you don't have to be Jonah to suffer shipwreck, you just need to have Jonah in your boat. Consequently, we cannot underestimate the power of aligning with the will of God in the place of prayer. When our prayers are aligned with God's will, they immediately take on the energy of a dangerous prayer.

The fourth critical component of a dangerous prayer is:

## 4. Perseverance in Prayer – Luke 18:1-4 (AMP)

> *Now Jesus was telling the disciples a parable to make the point that at all times they ought to pray and not give up and lose heart, saying, "In a certain city there was a judge who did not fear God and had no respect for man. There was a [desperate] widow in that city and she kept coming to him and saying, 'Give me justice and legal protection from my adversary.' For a time he would not; but later he said to himself, 'Even though I do not fear God nor respect man, yet because this widow continues to bother me, I will give her justice and legal protection;*

*otherwise by continually coming she [will be an intolerable annoyance and she] will wear me out.""*

In the parable of the persistent widow, Yeshua uses this parable to teach about the need for persistent prayer. The widow's unyielding approach to seeking justice is a metaphor for how believers should approach prayer. *We must not give up;* we should continuously seek and knock on the doors of Heaven's court until the answer we seek is fully materialized. I am sure there were days when the widow felt like giving up, especially due to the uncaring attitude of the judge who had the power to grant her the justice she so desperately needed.

I am saddened by how easily so many modern-day Christians give up on their prayers. This is the side effect of a culture where "lazy" has become a currency of social and technological engagement. While "lazy" has led to many amazing innovative technologies to meet the needs of the lazy, there exists no shortcut or microwave solution to knowing God intimately. This means God expects our culture of lazy people to still pay the price of seeking Him out of His hiding place just like the ancients did. This divine attitude and attribute places a premium on persistence in the place of prayer! Consequently, the persistent prayer is a dangerous prayer.

### 5. Confession and Repentance – Daniel 9:3-7 (NKJV)

*Then I set my face toward the Lord God to make request by prayer and supplications, with fasting, sackcloth, and ashes. And I prayed to the Lord my God, and made confession, and said, "O Lord, great and awesome God, who keeps His covenant and mercy with those who love Him, and with those who keep His commandments, we have sinned and committed iniquity, we have done wickedly and rebelled, even by departing from Your precepts and Your judgments. Neither have we heeded Your servants the prophets, who spoke in Your name to our kings and our princes, to our fathers and all the people of the land. O Lord, righteousness belongs to You, but to us shame of face, as it is this day—to the men of Judah, to the inhabitants of Jerusalem and all Israel, those near and those far off in all the countries to which You have driven them, because of the unfaithfulness which they have committed against You."*

Without a doubt, one of the greatest men of prayer in the Bible is Daniel. Daniel prayed for his people, *the Jews who were in captivity in Babylon and the remnant who remained in Jerusalem.* He started by confessing their sins and seeking divine mercy. Daniel's prayer in Daniel 9:3-7 is a profound example of the profound power of combining "confession and repentance." Daniel's prayer acknowledges human fallibility and the desperate need for divine mercy. Please take note that a prayer that begins with acknowledging one's sins and seeking forgiveness paves the way for a deeper and more honest relationship with God. Jesus alluded to the importance of "confession and repentance" in one of His famous parables:

*Also He spoke this parable to some who trusted in themselves that they were righteous, and despised others: "Two men went up to the temple to pray, one a Pharisee and the other a tax collector. The Pharisee stood and prayed thus with himself, 'God, I thank You that I am not like other men—extortioners, unjust, adulterers, or even as this tax collector. I fast twice a week; I give tithes of all that I possess.' And the tax collector, standing afar off, would not so much as raise his eyes to heaven, but beat his breast, saying, 'God, be merciful to me a sinner!' I tell you, this man went down to his house justified rather than the other; for everyone who exalts himself will be humbled, and he who humbles himself will be exalted"* (Luke 18:9-14 NKJV).

This parable in Luke 18 underscores the premium God places on a truly repentant heart that is quick to confess sin in order to get right with God. Yeshua also shows us the futility of a prideful spirit in prayer, which characterizes much of what I call "religious prayers." It's amazing how many so-called born-again Christians have their prayers infected with the spirit of religious pride. Especially those who are active proponents of the hyper-grace message—they treat heartfelt repenting after salvation like an unwanted baby. However, dangerous prayers are fueled through the hearts of those who are truly repentant and broken before the Lord.

## 6. A Practical Understanding of the Courts of Heaven – Luke 18:3-8 (AMP)

> *There was a [desperate] widow in that city and she kept coming to him and saying, "Give me justice and legal protection from my adversary." For a time he would not; but later he said to himself, "Even though I do not fear God nor respect man, yet because this widow continues to bother me, I will give her justice and legal protection; otherwise by continually coming she [will be an intolerable annoyance and she] will wear me out." Then the Lord said, "Listen to what the unjust judge says! And will not [our just] God defend and avenge His elect [His chosen ones] who cry out to Him day and night? Will He delay [in providing justice] on their behalf? I tell you that He will defend and avenge them quickly...."*

One of the cornerstone components for a dangerous prayer is a practical understanding of the courts of Heaven and how they affect believers in the place of prayer. In Luke 18:3-8, Yeshua shows us through the parable of the widow and the corrupt judge about how the courts of Heaven operate. In the parable Yeshua tells us that there was a desperate widow in a certain city with a ruthless adversary who was coming against her. It's clear that her adversary in the story was a legal opponent. Consequently, stopping her adversary from attacking her required legal action. She ran to the unrighteous judge who had legal jurisdiction over the territory where she and her adversary lived. According to Yeshua, the city judge was corrupt and did not care about the merits of her case, whatsoever.

Nevertheless, the woman's persistency in coming before the corrupt judge's court began to upset his peace of mind. In order to get back his peace of mind, he reluctantly gave her justice and legal protection from her adversary. Yeshua used this story as an allegory to point to a higher and superior court system—the courts of Heaven. The purpose of the parable was to highlight the legal nature of our adversary, satan. That he is not merely a street brawler, but an actual opponent at law in a very dynamic spiritual court, where he brings accusations and charges against the saints, day and night. This is why the dangerous decrees are designed to pass through the courts of Heaven in order to silence any legal rights satan has amassed against us. I am convinced that satan can never assault a child of God without a legal foothold. He needs to show "probable cause" before God, the Righteous Judge, can allow him to attack a child of God.

### 7. A Post-Prayer Posture of Thanksgiving – 1 Thessalonians 5:18 (AMP)

> In every situation [no matter what the circumstances] be thankful and continually give thanks to God; for this is the will of God for you in Christ Jesus.

What do you do after you have made the apostolic and prophetic decrees contained in this book? I ask this question because most prayer warriors don't know what to do with themselves after they have prayed the prayer of faith and said whatever needed to be said. In other words, how do you keep *faith alive* after you have prayed the prayer of faith? Answer: **You enter the amazing world of thanksgiving!**

Thanksgiving allows us to keep hope alive and hold onto the object of our faith until the complete manifestation of the things we have asked for in prayer. Thanksgiving is literally thanking God in advance for the things that we know He has already done by faith, but which our physical eyes have yet to see. Consequently, the dangerous prayers and decrees that are contained in this book conclude in the beautiful posture of thanksgiving to the Lord!

In conclusion, these seven biblical references, spanning both the Old and New Testaments, present a comprehensive view of what constitutes a biblically sound prayer. They collectively emphasize sincerity, faith, alignment with God's will, perseverance, the courts of Heaven, and the importance of confession and repentance. Such prayers, which are deeply rooted in spiritual truth and understanding, resonate with the heart of God and are likely to be answered within the economy of His infinite wisdom and timing. In the context of spiritual warfare, these dangerous prayers become powerful tools for the believer, providing strength, guidance, and assurance in the face of life's challenges.

# Life Application

## *Memory Verse*

> *This is the confidence we have in approaching God: that if we ask anything according to his will, he hears us. And if we know that he hears us—whatever we ask—we know that we have what we asked of him* (1 John 5:14-15 NIV).

## *Reflections*

1. What is the importance of thanksgiving in prayer?

   thanksgiving alots us to keep
   hope alive and whole on in
   our faith.

2. Why did the widow in Luke 18 go to see the corrupt judge?

   they was a certain widow in a city
   that ruthless adversary keep coming
   against her.

# CHAPTER 3

# Pulling Down
# Demonic Strongholds

For the weapons of our warfare are not carnal but mighty in God for pulling down strongholds, casting down arguments and every high thing that exalts itself against the knowledge of God, bringing every thought into captivity to the obedience of Christ, and being ready to punish all disobedience when your obedience is fulfilled (**2 Corinthians 10:4-6 NKJV**).

In the context of spiritual warfare and demonology, the concept of "pulling down strongholds" is a key component of what it takes to do spiritual warfare at a higher level. The anchor Scripture for this chapter is 2 Corinthians 10:4-6. In this passage, the apostle Paul speaks about the spiritual weapons given to believers to combat demonic forces in all their rankings. This chapter explores five biblical references that illuminate and illustrate the process and importance of dismantling these spiritual and demonic strongholds. As a matter of definition, *a spiritual stronghold is a habitual pattern of thought, built into a person's thought life.* Satan and his minions want to capture the minds of people: the mind is the citadel of the soul. Whoever controls the mind controls a very strategic place!

# A Biblical Approach to Spiritual Warfare

Any student of the Bible knows that the Bible is very clear about one critical thing—we are involved in a high stakes' spiritual warfare between the forces of darkness and the Kingdom of light. In other words, while we have holy angels on our side who are protecting us daily, there are also very malicious and evil spirits that want to destroy our life on earth. The ultimate prize sought by these malicious, demonic entities is to drag our souls to hell in the afterlife.

In the book of Ephesians, the apostle Paul was given a divine download about the structure and hierarchy of satan's kingdom and how it operates. For this reason, it is important for me to give you some highlights about the nature of the spiritual warfare we are engaged in and the critical elements to this warfare that ensure we will live a spiritually victorious life. We will examine the following critical elements to prevailing over the powers of darkness and pulling down demonic strongholds.

## *1. The Foundation of Spiritual Warfare – 2 Corinthians 10:4-5 (NIV)*

> *The weapons we fight with are not the weapons of the world. On the contrary, they have divine power to demolish strongholds. We demolish arguments and every pretension that sets itself up against the knowledge of God, and we take captive every thought to make it obedient to Christ.*

This passage in 2 Corinthians 10:4-5 lays the groundwork for understanding spiritual warfare. It emphasizes the fact that the battle against spiritual strongholds requires divine power, not earthly power. The strongholds mentioned here include false arguments, theories, philosophies and reasoning that oppose the truth contained in the Word of God. The key to overcoming the spiritual "strongholds of the mind" is to bring every thought into obedience to Christ, which means aligning our thinking with the Word of God as revealed in the holy Scriptures. What is clear from examining 2 Corinthians 10:4-5 is that the strongholds that we are fighting are primarily mental in nature. Satan knows that once he forms strongholds of demonically influenced thinking in our minds, we will quickly become captives or easy prey for the kingdom of darkness. Joyce Meyer calls this the "battlefield of the mind."

## 2. The Armor of God – Ephesians 6:12-18 (NIV)

> For our struggle is not against flesh and blood, but against... the spiritual forces of evil in the heavenly realms. Therefore put on the full armor of God...(Ephesians 6:12-13 NIV).

Ephesians 6:12-18 teaches that the true nature of our conflict is spiritual, not physical. In my walk of faith there is no passage that has been more helpful to me as a believer in Christ to understand the nature and dynamics of the spiritual warfare we face than the passage in Ephesians 6. The apostle Paul makes it very clear that our struggle or warfare is not against flesh and blood. This is why we can't get caught up fighting people when we are supposed to be fighting spirits.

The apostle Paul goes on to give us a prophetic narrative on the hierarchy of satan's demonic kingdom. It doesn't take a rocket scientist to figure out that that satan's kingdom is a well-oiled machine, hell-bent on one thing only—*to kill, steal, and destroy human souls.* Thankfully, in the same passage the apostle Paul gives us the antidote to defeating the fiery darts of the enemy by putting on the full armor of God. Paul goes on to say that the armor of God is real, and every believer needs to know how to put on the full armor of God to overcome the works of the enemy. The armor of God includes truth, righteousness, the gospel of peace, faith, salvation, the word of God, and prayer. These elements are essential in pulling down strongholds, as they equip believers with the necessary spiritual resources to stand against demonic influences.

## 3. Submission and Resistance – James 4:7 (NIV)

> *Submit yourselves, then, to God. Resist the devil, and he will flee from you.*

In James 4:7, we are confronted with one of the most important Kingdom principles for defeating evil and pulling down strongholds. According to James, the apostle and brother of Yeshua, the process of dealing with spiritual strongholds is twofold:

1. Submission to God and
2. Resistance to the devil

We can't defeat the devil if we don't understand this critical principle of submission. How can we rebuke the devil and his demonic minions when we ourselves are finding it difficult to submit our will to the will of God? So, what is submission in the context of James 4:7? Submission involves obedience to God and aligning one's life with His will. Failure to do so can only empower the demonic powers against us. Embracing the light is far more important than resisting the darkness.

After our submission to God has been fully vetted and approved in the courts of Heaven, we are ready to move on to the next part of this spiritual technology. The apostle James tells us that after we submit to God, we are fully empowered to rise in spiritual stature—and resist the devil. Under this spiritual atmosphere, satan will have no choice but to flee from us. What is resisting satan? Resistance is the active rejection of demonic influences over our minds. This dual approach ensures that we are ministering from a position of strength in our spiritual warfare with the powers of darkness.

## 4. The Power of Prayer and Fasting – Mark 9:29 (NKJV)

> *So He said to them, "This kind can come out by nothing but prayer and fasting."*

Without a doubt one of the most powerful spiritual technologies for pulling down strongholds and casting out demons is this spiritual practice of prayer and fasting. I call prayer and fasting the power twins of the Kingdom of God. Without exception, every man or woman whom God has used mightily in the Bible and our modern times happens to be a person of prayer and fasting. If we hope to be successful at pulling down strongholds and making prophetic decrees that are guaranteed to come to pass, we need to take the realm of prayer and fasting very seriously. In this passage in Mark 9, Yeshua addresses a demonic stronghold that was particularly resilient. He quickly indicates that some spiritual battles require not just prayer but also fasting. This combination intensifies the spiritual discipline needed to work miracles. Consequently, prayer and fasting brings us into a deeper level of spiritual authority and power. May I suggest that you embark on a period of fasting before you start making the dangerous decree prayers that are in the second part of this book.

## 5. Authority in Christ – Acts 16:16-18 (NASB1995)

> *...Paul...turned and said to the spirit, "I command you in the name of Jesus Christ to come out of her!" And it came out at that very moment.*

Another equally important spiritual tool that we have in our arsenal for pulling down strongholds is our authority in Christ. As born-again believers, we can activate the authority over principalities and powers that Jesus's death and shed blood purchased for us on the Cross. The Bible is very clear that we are not hopeless individuals chasing our tails in life. We are children of the Most High, with access to some of the most amazing weaponry the Kingdom of God has to offer. However, none of that tramples the fact that Yeshua gave us the right to exercise authority in the Kingdom. We need to use our God-given authority in Christ Jesus to rebuke every demonic entity trying to build a stronghold in our minds. Acts 16:16-18, demonstrates the authority believers have in Christ to confront demonic forces. Paul's direct command in the name of Yeshua emphasizes the power vested in Yeshua's name. It is a clear example of how believers can actively confront and dismantle demonic strongholds through the authority Christ has given us.

## 6. The Word of God – Hebrews 4:12 (NKJV)

> *For the word of God is living and powerful, and sharper than any two-edged sword, piercing even to the division of soul and spirit, and of joints and marrow, and is a discerner of the thoughts and intents of the heart.*

Within the economy of glory there is nothing more powerful at destroying strongholds, casting out devils, and manifesting the Kingdom of God than the Word of God. The Word of God above all else is the most potent weapon we have against the powers of darkness and many of the secular philosophies that want to infiltrate our minds to weaken our faith. The writer of the book of Hebrews makes it very clear that the Word of God, the Bible, is living, and that it is powerful, and that it is sharper than any two-edged sword. Why? It's because it pierces both the soul and spirit, all the way to the division of soul and spirit. It is no wonder that when Yeshua was on a 40-day fast, He used this expression several times to deal with satan, *"It is written."* Yeshua used this expression on the mountain of temptation to defeat satan and pull down every stronghold satan was trying to legislate. If we are failing to say, "It is written" when we are fasting, we are making a big mistake. The Word of God must be our number-one anchor in our spiritual battle with the powers of darkness and in pulling down strongholds.

In closing, "pulling down strongholds" in the spiritual realm is a crucial aspect of a believer's life. It requires the understanding that the battle is spiritual and calls for divine power. The Scriptures collectively highlight the importance of using God-given spiritual weapons—faith, truth, righteousness, the Word of God, prayer, fasting, and the authority of Jesus Christ. These tools enable you to effectively confront and dismantle the strongholds of false reasoning, demonic influence, and spiritual opposition—leading to a victorious Christian life.

# Life Application

## *Memory Verse*

> *For the weapons of our warfare are not carnal but mighty in God for pulling down strongholds, casting down arguments and every high thing that exalts itself against the knowledge of God, bringing every thought into captivity to the obedience of Christ, and being ready to punish all disobedience when your obedience is fulfilled* (2 Corinthians 10:4-6 NKJV).

## *Reflections*

1. What is a stronghold?

_____

_____

_____

_____

2. What are the 4 of the 7 critical elements of spiritual warfare?

_____

_____

_____

_____

CHAPTER 4

# The Believer's Authority

But you will receive power and ability when the Holy Spirit comes
upon you; and you will be My witnesses [to tell people about Me]
both in Jerusalem and in all Judea, and Samaria, and even to the
ends of the earth (**Acts 1:8 AMP**).

I t is important to note that on His way out, right before the ascension
from the Mount of Olives into the heavenly realms from whence He
came, the Lord Jesus Christ admonished His disciples that they were not
to rush into public ministry until they had been endowed with power from
on high. Yeshua's admonition to His disciples, many of them had already
spent over three years with Him, is a clear indication that we cannot challenge the demonic powers armed with human philosophies. The devil will
run us out of town with shame on our faces if we try to deal with demonic
entities without the backing of spiritual power.

It seems to me that in the realm of spirits, "power" is the only thing that
demons and fallen angels respect. In this regard it becomes vitally important for believers to understand their God-given authority and power over
the demonic entities in the spirit world. Jesus made it clear that once they
received power from on high, they would become witnesses of His resur-
rection. This is why Christianity was never designed to be a toothless and
powerless religion.

# The Believer's Authority in Christ: A Biblical Exploration

The concept of the believer's authority in Christ is a foundational aspect of Christian faith, particularly in the realms of spiritual warfare and demonology. This authority stems from the relationship between believers and Christ, enabling them to act in His name. This chapter explores this authority using Genesis 1:26-27, Luke 10:19, and Mark 16:15-18 as anchor Scriptures. I further supplement these anchor Scriptures with five additional biblical references. It's imperative that we grow in the consciousness of our spiritual authority in Christ before we can make powerful decrees that destroy strongholds.

> *Then God said, "Let Us make man in Our image, according to Our likeness; let them have dominion over the fish of the sea, over the birds of the air, and over the cattle, over all the earth and over every creeping thing that creeps on the earth." So God created man in His own image; in the image of God He created him; male and female He created them* (Genesis 1:26-27 NKJV).

This Genesis 1 passage is the beginning and foundation of man's God-given dominion. It establishes man as the delegated authority of God in the earth realm. The passage describes the creation of mankind in God's image and likeness. It highlights the inherent authority given to mankind over the earth. This authority is inherent in all people, saved or unsaved. However, it sets the stage for understanding our restored authority in Christ Jesus.

When Jesus died on the Cross and rose from the dead, He restored our authority over the planet and also increased the sphere of our authority by including things in "heavenly places" within the context of that authority. This means that the authority of the believer is an octave higher than the original dominion mandate that was given to Adam and Eve in Genesis chapter 1. The dominion (authority) God gave to Adam and Eve never included authority over "things" in heavenly places and under the earth. So, when we are making decrees to destroy demonic strongholds, our authority in Christ is superior to anything Adam ever had.

## Trampling on Serpents and Scorpions

> *I have given you authority* to trample on snakes and scorpions and to overcome all the power of the enemy; nothing will harm you (Luke 10:19 NIV).

This direct statement from Christ establishes the believer's authority over demonic forces. Luke 10:19 is one of my favorite verses for feasting on the promise of the "believers' authority" through our union with Christ Jesus. In Luke 10:19 Yeshua makes it very clear that He has given us authority. The word *authority* comes from the Greek word *exousia,* which literally means the "right to exercise power." Jesus has given us the right to exercise and demonstrate God's power—that is authority!

Jesus goes on to describe the scope of that authority. We find out that it comes with *the ability to trample on serpents and scorpions and to overcome all the power of the enemy.* And the icing on the cake is that we get to walk away from a spiritual warfare without being afraid of being casualties of the demonic powers. The terminology "snakes and scorpions" is a metaphor for different ranks of demonic entities that we have the power to overcome. This is why when you start making dangerous decrees, I encourage you to do so with boldness, assured of your authority in Christ Jesus over demonic powers.

# The Authority of the Believer in the Great Commission

*And He said to them, "Go into all the world and preach the gospel to every creature. He who believes and is baptized will be saved; but he who does not believe will be condemned. And these signs will follow those who believe: In My name they will cast out demons; they will speak with new tongues; they will take up serpents; and if they drink anything deadly, it will by no means hurt them; they will lay hands on the sick, and they will recover"* (Mark 16:15-18 NKJV).

One of the most important apostolic commissions Jesus gifted to His disciples and His global church is crystallized in the great commission found in the two Gospels, Mark and Matthew. I quickly want to examine these two passages of Scripture to mine them for gold nuggets related to the authority of the believer in Christ Jesus. In Mark 16:15-18, Jesus commands all His disciples to go into the world and preach the gospel to every creature. Then He proceeds to break down what we are authorized to do within the great commission. As you read the following list, ask yourself the question: "With this kind of authority, how can I fail to win?"

- We have the authority to baptize people in His name.

- We have the authority to cast out devils (demons).

- We have the authority to speak in new tongues or heavenly language.

- We have the authority to take up serpents and remove them from people's lives.

> *All authority in heaven and on earth has been given to me.*
> *Therefore go and make disciples of all nations...* (Matthew
> 28:18-19 NIV).

The passage from Matthew 28:18-19, underscores that Jesus's authority extends over Heaven and earth, to even include the underworld. Yeshua's command for His disciples to make disciples and baptize nations in the name of the eternal Godhead implies that His "all authority" is shared with His followers, empowering them to act on His behalf. I want you to imagine this authority backing you up every time you make apostolic and prophetic decrees.

## Authority in the Armor of God

> *Finally, be strong in the Lord and in his mighty power. Put on*
> *the full armor of God, so that you can take your stand against*
> *the devil's schemes* (Ephesians 6:10-11 NIV).

In Ephesians 6:10-12, the apostle Paul opens another mystery that unlocks the believer's authority in Christ Jesus. This mystery is called the *full armor of God*. Paul declares to the Ephesians that they can afford to be strong in the Lord and in the power of His might by putting on the *full armor of God*. Built within the supernatural technology of the *full armor of God* is the ability to stand against all the schemes of the devil and quench every fiery dart that comes from the demonic kingdom. This is similar to "Superman" putting on his Superman suit, which enabled him to transform from the ordinary Clark Kent to the mighty Superman! In other words, there was inherent authority and superpowers built within the technology of Superman's suit.

This is how *the full armor of God* operates for believers who take the time to put it on before they begin to do battle in the spirit. I advise that before you begin to make the dangerous decrees contained in this book, ask the Lord to put on you *the full armor of God*. This passage encourages believers to be equipped with God's armor so they can stand firm against spiritual forces of evil. *The implication is that believers have the authority to stand against demonic powers, protected and empowered by God Himself.*

## The Promise of Doing Greater Works

> *Very truly I tell you, whoever believes in me will do the works I have been doing, and they will do even greater things than these, because I am going to the Father* (John 14:12 NIV).

The believer's authority in Christ is further compounded by *the promise of doing greater works* that Jesus gifted to His disciples. This means that God committed Himself to work through us via the Person of the Holy Spirit to do *greater works* than the ones Jesus performed when He was on earth. This dimension of power and authority is made possible by the fact that Jesus our High Priest has already ascended to the right hand of God. As your eternal royal High Priest after the Order of Melchizedek, Yeshua is interceding for you to operate in this dimension of power and authority. In John 14:12-14, Jesus promises that believers will perform works greater than His own, *implying a greater transfer of authority.*

## The Promise of the Holy Spirit

> *But you will receive power when the Holy Spirit comes on you; and you will be my witnesses...* (Acts 1:8 NIV).

The arrival of the Holy Spirit after the day of Pentecost signifies the empowerment of believers. This power includes the authority to be Christ's witnesses in every sphere of human enterprise. The scope of this authority is all encompassing. It includes the ability to act in His authority worldwide. The arrival of the Holy Spirit and His ability to be omnipresent brought about the universality of this authority.

> *You, dear children, are from God and have overcome them, because the one who is in you is greater than the one who is in the world* (1 John 4:4 NIV).

The promise of the indwelling presence of the Holy Spirit further deepened the wells of Christ's authority in every believer. First John 4:4 clearly affirms that the indwelling presence of God in all believers grants them superiority over worldly and demonic forces. It's a clear indication of the authority believers possess through their union with Christ. The Holy Spirit in us equals indwelling authority. It doesn't get better than this.

In closing, the believer's authority in Christ is a profound and empowering biblical truth. It's deeply rooted in the believer's identity in Christ and is manifested through the Holy Spirit's indwelling presence. This indwelling authority enables believers to exercise dominion over demonic powers, carry out Christ's great commission, and perform greater works in His name. It's essential for effective spiritual warfare and for the advancement of God's Kingdom on earth. Understanding and exercising this authority is pivotal for every believer in their spiritual journey of faith.

# Life Application

## *Memory Verse*

> *Very truly I tell you, whoever believes in me will do the works I have been doing, and they will do even greater things than these, because I am going to the Father* (John 14:12 NIV).

## *Reflections*

1. How does the promise of the Holy Spirit affect every believer?

_____

_____

_____

_____

2. In Luke 10:19 what is included in the authority Christ gave to His disciples?

_____

_____

_____

_____

# CHAPTER 5

# Dissolving Satan's Legal Rights

Come to terms quickly [at the earliest opportunity] with your opponent at law [adversary] while you are with him [satan] on the way [to court], so that your opponent does not hand you over to the judge, and the judge to the guard, and you are thrown into prison. I assure you and most solemnly say to you, you will not come out of there until you have paid the last cent (**Matthew 5:25-26 AMP**).

The concept of the "Courts of Heaven" is a metaphorical interpretation used to understand how believers can engage in spiritual warfare and counteract satan's accusations within the framework of a very robust, supernatural, and heavenly judicial system. The concept of the courts of Heaven involves the idea of presenting cases before a divine tribunal (see Job 2:1-3), seeking justice and the nullification of the adversary's claims against us.

This chapter explores this theme using specific biblical references to elucidate how believers can dissolve satan's legal rights against them. In the context of this writing, it is important that we pass through the courts of heaven before we begin to make the dangerous decrees that are contained in the oracle of this book. This is because we do not want to make dangerous decrees to dislodge demonic strongholds when satan has legal rights to resist or assail us.

## The Accuser in the Divine Council

> One day the members of the heavenly court came again
> to present themselves before the Lord, and the Accuser,
> Satan, came with them. "Where have you come from?" the
> Lord asked Satan. Satan answered the Lord, "I have been
> patrolling the earth, watching everything that's going on."
> Then the Lord asked Satan, "Have you noticed my servant
> Job? He is the finest man in all the earth. He is blameless—a
> man of complete integrity. He fears God and stays away from
> evil. And he has maintained his integrity, even though you
> urged me to harm him without cause." Satan replied to the
> Lord, "Skin for skin! A man will give up everything he has
> to save his life. But reach out and take away his health, and
> he will surely curse you to your face!" "All right, do with him
> as you please," the Lord said to Satan. "But spare his life"
> (Job 2:1-6 NLT).

In Job 2:1-6, satan appears before God and the heavenly court to accuse
Job. This passage illustrates the concept of a divine judicial council where
accusations against believers are presented and adjudicated. Job's experience
demonstrates that satan seeks to undermine the righteousness of believers by
bring up our flaws and shortcomings. However, the passage also reveals that
God sets limits on satan's activities, based upon a judicial process of "due
process" that he must abide by, within the heavenly judicial realm.

The good news is that we as believers in Christ, have the legal rights by
the blood of Jesus to step into this dimension of the courts of Heaven. We
can also present our case before the judicial council of Heaven and remind
God of the finished work of Yeshua and the promises of mercy and forgiveness that are littered throughout Scripture for us to silence the voice of
the accuser in the courts of Heaven. This enables us to demolish any legal

foothold that satan had against us that he could have used to resist the force of our prayers. This is why I have drafted every dangerous decree in Part Two of this book in such way as to satisfy the demands of the courts of Heaven in our time of prayer.

## The Ancient of Days and the Court's Judgment

> *I watched as thrones were put in place and the Ancient One sat down to judge. His clothing was as white as snow, his hair like purest wool. He sat on a fiery throne with wheels of laz-ing fire, and a river of fire was pouring out, flowing from his presence. Millions of angels ministered to him; many millions stood to attend him.* **Then the court began its session, and the books were opened** (Daniel 7:9-10 NLT).

> *He will defy the Most High and oppress the holy people of the Most High. He will try to change their sacred festivals and laws, and they will be placed under his control for a time, times, and half a time. But then* **the court will pass judg-ment**, *and all his power will be taken away and completely destroyed* (Daniel 7:25-26 NLT).

In the above Scriptural passages, the prophet Daniel is given a vision of God (as the Ancient of Days) and of a heavenly court that passes judgment. Daniel's prophetic vision depicts a court setting in heaven where judgments are rendered against the forces of evil, symbolized by the *"little horn"* speaking boastfully (see Daniel 7:8). This amazing prophetic vision represents God's divine courtroom as the ultimate authority over all earthly judicial systems and spiritual powers. This is truly exhalating!

When we understand how to effectively operate from the courts of Heaven, our judicial decrees against the demonic powers will take on a different meaning and vibration. Our confidence will soar because we know that God's supreme court is the ultimate authority over all demonic and human power centers. The expression, *"then the court began its session, and the books were opened,"* opens another powerful mystery and dimension of the courts of Heaven. When the heavenly court is in session it triggers the opening of *"the books."* This begs the question, what books are these? I believe these are the *books of destiny,* the *book of remembrance* and *Torah.* Some of these books are mentioned in Psalm 139 and Malachi 4.

The opening of these books tilts the courts of Heaven in our favor, as God the Righteous Judge is more likely to render a verdict based on what He wrote about our destiny *"from before the foundation of the world."* We can petition the Righteous Judge, who is also our blessed heavenly Father, to cancel and nullify all of satan's accusations and charges based on what is written about us in these scrolls from eternity. In addition to this, we can present Scriptures such as Romans 8:1-2 and 1 John 1:9 as part of our petition for divine clemency and acquittal from all of satan's accusations. You must remember that the main purpose for coming before the courts of Heaven is to provide our Righteous Judge a legal basis based upon Scripture to dissolve all of satan's charges of wrongful doing against us.

## Silencing the Accuser!

> *Then I heard a loud voice in heaven, saying, "Now the salvation, and the power, and the kingdom (dominion, reign) of our God, and the authority of His Christ have come; for the accuser of our [believing] brothers and sisters has been thrown down [at last], he who accuses them and keeps bringing*

*charges [of sinful behavior] against them before our God day
and night. And they overcame and conquered him because of
the blood of the Lamb and because of the word of their testimony, for they did not love their life and renounce their faith
even when faced with death* (Revelation 12:10-11 AMP).

This passage in Revelation 12:10-11 is one of my favorite anchor Scriptures
for silencing our arch accuser in the courts of Heaven. Revelation 12:10-
11 shows the ultimate casting down of the accuser (satan) and the eternal
victory of the saints. This passage at close introspection describes the tri-
umph of the saints over satan and his kingdom through the shed blood of
the Lamb and the word of their testimony. This passage clearly demonstrates
that all of satan's legal claims and accusations can be nullified through the
redemptive work of Christ and the believer's testimony.

It's interesting to note that the word *testimony* is a judicial word. It's not
a religious terminology. It's a word forged within the framework of law.
Within a judicial context, a *testimony* is a judicial record of an eyewitness
account to matters or cases that are relevant to a particular court proceeding.

From reading Revelation 12:10-11, we quickly see three spiritual weapons that all believers can activate to defeat satan and silence all his accusations. Namely:

1. The shed blood of the Lamb.
2. The believer's testimony about the finished work of Yeshua
   and the miracles they have personally experienced.
3. The believer's willingness to go die for the sake of the One who
   died for them on the Cross.

We must never forget that under the New Testament, post the resurrec-
tion of Yeshua from the dead, satan's real power is the "power of accusation." If you don't think that accusations have real power and sting, then

you are very fortunate that you have never been on the receiving end of false accusations.

One of my favorite TV programs is watching shows about the Innocence Project, which brings to life the real-life stories of men and women who spent decades behind bars because of a false accusation—only to be fully exonerated by DNA evidence. In the judicial system, the engines of justice don't begin to turn until someone has been accused or charged. So, every time satan brings a railing accusation against us in the courts of Heaven, he triggers a court proceeding in the spirit world against us. This doesn't mean that every time satan accuses us before God we must appear before the courts of Heaven. In most cases many of satan's accusations are quickly dissolved by the voice of the blood of Jesus, which continuously cleanses us from all sin if *we walk in the light as He is in the light* (1 John 1:7).

However, there are times—quite often for some believers who have not yet learned the covenant of total obedience—when satan's accusation (charge) against a believer is based on "active rebellion" against God's Word or the leading of the Holy Spirit. In such cases "sin" is no longer just the *missing of the mark*, it morphs into an active insurrection against God's authority. Such a spiritual insurrection is not covered by the tenets of 1 John 1:7. To be absorbed of these willful acts of rebellion we need to sorrowfully acknowledge our transgression before God in heartfelt repentance. This is when we must appear before the courts of Heaven and confess our transgression according to 1 John 1:9. Failure to do so causes satan to win default judgments against us in the courts of Heaven. This scenario is one of the reasons an awareness of the realities of the courts of Heaven proves very helpful to believers. There have been times the Lord has summoned me into the courts of Heaven "by revelation" to answer and silence the voice of the accuser.

# Christ Our Advocate

*...If anybody does sin, we have an advocate with the Father—*
*Jesus Christ, the Righteous One* (1 John 2:1 NIV).

First John 2:1 clearly suggests that Jesus acts as a legal advocate for believers. We know that within the judicial system, an advocate is an officer of the court who champions the innocence and legal rights of the defendant or accused. In other words, an advocate is a defense lawyer, barrister, or attorney who represents the accused. In the heavenly court, Christ's advocacy ensures the dismissal of charges against believers, based on His atoning sacrifice. This is what makes entering the courts of Heaven very exciting. Our Advocate is the second member of the eternal Godhead, our High Priest and Savior who paid the ultimate price for our redemption. How can we fail to win cases against satan in such a courtroom if we are sincere in our repentance?

Once we are successful at prevailing on the courts of Heaven to dismiss all of satan's charges, there is no decree we make that won't come to pass. Romans 8:33 (NIV) boldly declares, *"Who will bring any charge against those whom God has chosen? It is God who justifies."* This passage reassures us that no accusation against believers will stand in the divine courtroom, as God Himself is the One who justifies them. This passage reflects the ultimate nullification of satan's legal rights against believers.

# Life Application

## *Memory Verse*

> *Then I heard a loud voice in heaven, saying, "Now the salvation, and the power, and the kingdom (dominion, reign) of our God, and the authority of His Christ have come; for the accuser of our [believing] brothers and sisters has been thrown down [at last], he who accuses them and keeps bringing charges [of sinful behavior] against them before our God day and night. And they overcame and conquered him because of the blood of the Lamb and because of the word of their testimony, for they did not love their life and renounce their faith even when faced with death"* (Revelation 12:10-11 AMP).

## *Reflections*

1. What are some of the books that are opened when the court is seated?

   _____

   _____

   _____

   _____

2.  What is satan's number-one weapon against believers in the courts of Heaven?

_____

_____

_____

_____

# CHAPTER 6

# The Courts of Heaven and Judicial Decrees

Woe to those who decree unrighteous decrees, who write misfortune, which they have prescribed to rob the needy of justice, and to take what is right from the poor of My people, that widows may be their prey, and that they may rob the fatherless. What will you do in the day of punishment, and in the desolation which will come from afar? To whom will you flee for help? And where will you leave your glory? (Isaiah 10:1-3 NKJV)

There exists a symbiotic relationship between the courts of Heaven and the power of judicial decrees. This symbiotic relationship is a concept rooted in biblical theology, emphasizing God's divine justice system and God's sovereign rule over earthly and spiritual matters. *A judicial decree is an official edict of the court backed by the force and rule of law.* We will shortly examine judicial decrees that were issued by the courts of Heaven through angelic or human officers of the court and their far-reaching spiritual implications.

## The Judgment of Unjust Judges

In Isaiah 10:1-3, the prophet Isaiah, acting as an officer of the heavenly court, condemns those corrupt kings and judges who decree unjust laws and oppress the poor. This passage of Scripture reveals the heavenly court's superior role in holding earthly rulers and judges accountable for their actions. It underscores the principle that all human authority is subject to divine scrutiny and judgment.

The concept of the courts of Heaven is evident here, as it is God who ultimately judges the actions of political and judicial leaders, ensuring justice and righteousness for all. For instance, the recent decrees in the United States forcing the public to receive and acknowledge transgenderism and all its mind-bending nuances is an example of oppressive and demonically engineered judicial decrees. People are being forced by the force of law to lie to their own eyes and the laws of nature, by being forced to believe that a man with a penis can become a woman in the twinkling of an eye, by simply declaring themselves as a woman. The immutable fact that God created a world of men with two unchangeable genders (male and female, Genesis 1:27) has been thrown to the wind of perpetual idiocrasy.

## The Decree of the Watchers

*I saw in the visions of my head while on my bed, and there was a watcher, a holy one, coming down from heaven. He cried aloud and said thus: "Chop down the tree and cut off its branches, strip off its leaves and scatter its fruit. Let the beasts get out from under it, and the birds from its branches. Nevertheless leave the stump and roots in the earth, bound with a band of iron and bronze, in the tender grass of the field. Let* *it be wet with the dew of heaven, and let him graze with the beasts on the grass of the earth. Let his heart be changed from that of a man, let him be given the heart of a beast, and let seven times pass over him. This decision is by **the decree of the watchers**, and the sentence by the word of the holy ones, in order that the living may know that the Most High rules in the kingdom of men, gives it to whomever He will, and sets over it the lowest of men"* (Daniel 4:13-17 NKJV).

Without a doubt this passage in Daniel 4:13-17 is one of the most powerful biblical demonstrations of the power of judicial decrees enacted by the courts of Heaven. It involves the king of one of the most powerful Babylonian empires that ever existed. To the outside observer, this mighty kingdom of King Nebuchadnezzar would never fall nor it's majestic dominion interrupted. Without warning and much fanfare King Nebuchadnezzar had a profound vision in a dream of the night. In the dream, King Nebuchadnezzar saw a "watcher," a holy one, coming down from Heaven to pronounce judgment.

This decree, described as a decision by the watchers and the holy ones, indicates a collective judicial decision in the heavenly realm against him. It demonstrates the power of divine decrees and the courts of Heaven's authority over earthly kingdoms, emphasizing that God's dominion is the ultimate dominion. The prophet Daniel who loved the king was very disturbed by the actual meaning of the dream. It took him a while to recover emotionally before he could interpret the meaning of the dream. When Daniel finally interpreted the dream, he made it clear to King Nebuchadnezzar that he had offended a superior court in the heavenly realm, and a decree or sentence had been passed over him. He was going to be driven away from the world of men to live with the beasts of the field. The decree or sentence was for seven years! In other words, the heavenly court was sending him to prison to "do time" just like any other prisoner.

The very fact that the courts of Heaven can imprison a person on earth demonstrates its utter superiority over the courts of men. Daniel immediately went into lawyer mode. He advised the king to repent and to show mercy and treat the poor righteously, and perhaps there could be a lessening of his sentence. In the natural judicial system, this legal strategy Daniel employed is known as *appealing to the mercy of the court to mitigate the harshness of the sentence that can come from the presiding judge over the case.* Good lawyers use this legal strategy a lot, especially if their client is a first-time offender.

Unfortunately, King Nebuchadnezzar did not listen to Daniel's wise counsel. I believe King Nebuchadnezzar did not believe that an invisible heavenly court could do to him what his political enemies had failed to do. So, one day while he was walking on the roof of his palace to gaze upon and pride himself in the majesty of his glorious empire, the decree of the watchers came upon him. While the words of praising himself were still in his mouth, a watcher audibly pronounced his sentence that the prophet Daniel had already deciphered.

In the twinkling of an eye, the king lost his mind and gained the mind of a beast of the wild. He was quickly driven away from the throne of Babylon and was driven into the wild, like any other animal. He would retain the mind of a wild beast for exactly seven years according to the decree or sentence of the watchers from God's heavenly courtroom. This is why the prayers in this book *all pass through the courts of Heaven,* so that they can carry the judicial power of this superior heavenly court. This is why this book is titled, *Dangerous Decrees That Destroy Strongholds.*

# A King's Decree Reflecting Heavenly Justice

*I make a decree that in every dominion of my kingdom men must tremble and fear before the God of Daniel. For He is the living God, and steadfast forever; His kingdom is the one which shall not be destroyed, and His dominion shall endure to the end* (Daniel 6:26 NKJV).

Saying that King Darius loved Daniel is truly an understatement. The king loved him deeply because there was no one in his entire kingdom he could trust like Daniel. However, some jealous nobles within the kingdom of Darius wanted to destroy Daniel's position of favor in the king's life. So, they seduced the unsuspecting king to issue an edict (a decree) that would require people in Persia within a period of 24 hours not to worship any other god except the king. The king did not know the decree he had just signed into law was weaponized to destroy his best friend, Daniel! Daniel's enemies had malicious intentions because they knew that Daniel was inseparable from his God. He prayed to his God daily!

As soon as the edict went into motion, the enemies of Daniel went to Daniel's house to see if he would obey the king's edict. They quickly ran to the king to accuse Daniel of insubordination to the king's edict. When King Darius realized he had been fooled by his nobles to issue his unrighteous decree, he panicked and all appetite for food left him. He called all the wise legal minds of the Persian empire to see if there was a way to deliver Daniel from his royal edict, but they failed to find a way to change the unchangeable edict of a king of Persia. Daniel was reluctantly thrown into the lions' den, while the king spent the rest of the night praying and fasting for a divine intervention by Daniel's God.

God did not disappoint neither Daniel nor the deceived king. God miraculously delivered Daniel from the mouths of the hungry lions. King Darius, after witnessing Daniel's deliverance from the lions' den, issued another "decree" that people in the Persian empire must fear and reverence the God of Daniel. *This final decree aligned King Darius with the heavenly court's decisions, showing once again that when earthly rulers align with divine justice, their decrees can reflect heavenly principles and power.* This instance illustrates the interaction between heavenly decrees and earthly governance.

## Nineveh's King Aligns with God's Decree

> *And he caused it to be proclaimed and published throughout Nineveh by the decree of the king and his nobles, saying, Let neither man nor beast, herd nor flock, taste anything; do not let them eat, or drink water* (Jonah 3:7 NKJV).

In Jonah 3:7, the king of Nineveh issues a decree for fasting and repentance in response to Jonah's prophecy of national destruction. This act of submission to God's warning demonstrates how divine decrees can influence and alter the course of human actions and decisions. This is why the book you are holding in your hands is titled, *Dangerous Decrees That Destroy Strongholds*. The king of Nineveh's decree in obedience to God's prophetic message highlights the power of divine justice and mercy when acknowledged by earthly authorities. The decree the king made, coupled with heartfelt repentance and fasting, moved God and surprised the prophet Jonah. Jonah did everything in his power to run away from this assignment.

## The Boundaries Set by God's Decree

> *"Do you not fear Me?" says the Lord. "Will you not tremble at My presence, who have placed the sand as the bound*

*of the sea, by a perpetual decree, that it cannot pass beyond it? And though its waves toss to and fro, yet they cannot prevail; Though they roar, yet they cannot pass over it"* (Jeremiah 5:22 NKJV).

The realm of heavenly judicial decrees goes further than we realize. Impacting and affecting the laws of nature. Jeremiah 5:22 speaks of God setting boundaries for the sea by His decree, a metaphor illustrating God's sovereign control over nature and the established order. This verse from the book of Jeremiah represents the cosmic order as part of God's judicial authority, where His decrees have both physical and moral implications. It symbolizes the overarching power of God's judicial decisions in the courts of Heaven over all creation. This is why in Part Two "The Book of Dangerous Decrees," also included are decrees designed to manipulate the laws of nature and challenge the natural order of things.

In closing the concept of the courts of Heaven and the power of judicial decrees, the Bible demonstrates God's supreme authority and the interaction of divine justice with earthly matters. The passages of Scripture we have examined with forensic aptitude collectively highlight the importance of aligning human actions and laws with God's divine will and the ultimate accountability we all have to His heavenly court. This theme serves as a reminder of the balance between divine sovereignty and human responsibility in the pursuit of justice and righteousness. The powers of darkness are no match for this divinely inspired judicial system.

## Life Application

### *Memory Verse*

> *I make a decree that in every dominion of my kingdom men must tremble and fear before the God of Daniel. For He is the living God, and steadfast forever; His kingdom is the one which shall not be destroyed, and His dominion shall endure to the end* (Daniel 6:26 NKJV).

### *Reflections*

1. What sentence (decree) did the watchers pass on King Nebuchadnezzar?

   _____

   _____

   _____

   _____

2. How did the decree of King Darius affect Daniel?

   _____

   _____

   _____

   _____

# PART TWO

# The Book of Dangerous Decrees & Activation Prayers

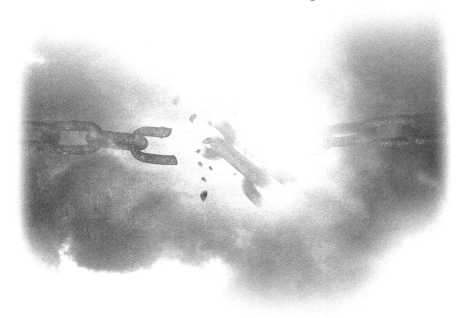

*O earth, earth, earth,*

*Hear the word of the Lord!*

*Thus says the Lord:*

*"Write this man down as childless,*

*A man who shall not prosper in his days;*

*For none of his descendants shall prosper,*

*Sitting on the throne of David,*

*And ruling anymore in Judah."*

**(Jeremiah 22:29-30 NKJV)**

# CHAPTER 7

# The Book of Dangerous Decrees

Then Hilkiah the high priest said to Shaphan the scribe, "I have found the Book of the Law in the house of the Lord." And Hilkiah gave the book to Shaphan, and he read it. So Shaphan the scribe went to the king, bringing the king word, saying, "Your servants have gathered the money that was found in the house, and have delivered it into the hand of those who do the work, who oversee the house of the Lord." Then Shaphan the scribe showed the king, saying, "Hilkiah the priest has given me a book." And Shaphan read it before the king. Now it happened, when the king heard the words of the Book of the Law, that he tore his clothes (**2 Kings 22:8-11 NKJV**).

What would you do if you stumbled upon a book containing dangerous decrees and proclamations that can change your life? Would you start using them? If you are wired like me, the answer to the last question is an absolute, "Yes!" This is exactly what happened to the young and highly impressionable King Josiah. When the young king by divine providence raised money and commissioned the renovations of the temple of God, it had a supernatural ripple effect. It was a ripple that would forever change his life and enshrine his legacy among the righteous kings of Israel.

During the process of cleaning and renovating the temple, the builders discovered an ancient parchment of the Torah, which contained a very unusual prophecy about King Josiah, connecting him to a prophet he had never met. When Hilkiah, the presiding high priest at the time, saw this ancient parchment and the prophecy it contained, he was rendered speechless. He knew this ancient parchment of the Torah, which had been collecting dust for many years in a temple left in ruins, had to quickly get to the young king.

> *Then Shaphan the scribe showed the king, saying, "Hilkiah the priest has given me a book." And Shaphan read it before the king. Now it happened, when the king heard the words of the Book of the Law, that he tore his clothes* (2 Kings 22:10-11 NKJV).

What a reaction to the reading of the Torah! What in God's name did Shaphan the scribe read that caused such a profound reaction by the young king? The young king tore his royal robes, which in ancient times was a symbol of a radical transition and personal transformation. Unbeknown to King Josiah, about a hundred years before he was born, God in His infinite intelligence sent a "nameless man of God" to Bethel (1 Kings 13) to confront an evil national altar and priesthood, which was corrupting the nation of Israel.

The nameless "man of God" had come to Bethel as an officer of the courts of Heaven to render a judgment on earth, which had already been rendered in the heavenly courtroom. It was a judgment against the evil national altar at Bethel. During this prophetic confrontation with the nameless man of God, the evil altar *"split apart"* and its ashes were poured out in a powerful demonstration of the power of God.

While judging the evil altar at Bethel the nameless man of God began to prophesy, shouting, *"O altar, altar! This is what the Lord says: A child named Josiah will be born into the dynasty of David. On you he will sacrifice the priests from the pagan shrines who come here to burn incense, and human bones will be burned on you"* (1 Kings 13:2 NLT). This was decreed 100 years before the birth of the young king! It is no wonder the young king was deeply moved. Wouldn't you be moved if you discovered that God had been speaking about you and your eternal ordination long before you were even born? Talk about the "force of manifest destiny" coursing through your veins. Josiah could hardly believe his ears. The almighty God knew him! That intimately? Wow!

Most importantly, the prophecy on the ancient parchment of the Torah awakened King Josiah's eternal ordination and mantle for national cleansing and reformation. He became king when he was only eight years old. His evil queen mother ruled the nation for ten years, even though King Josiah sat on the throne. He was mere a figurehead without real power. Meanwhile, his queen mother kept in place the very evil altars and worship of strange gods that he was called to destroy through his eternal ordination. Of course, the ancient prophecy changed everything!

King Josiah realized that he was tolerating what he was called to destroy. From that moment of onward, King Josiah became an instrument of trans-formation and national cleansing in the hands of the mighty God. He destroyed every evil altar in the land and killed the demonic priesthood behind it. Blood began to flow in the streets of Jerusalem; *it was the blood of those who attended to strange gods.* In the same manner, *"Welcome to the Book of Dangerous Decrees from the courts of Heaven that destroy strongholds."* May the following prayers be as transformation for you as discovering the ancient parchment of the Torah was for King Josiah.

## Life Application

### *Memory Verse*

> *Then Hilkiah the high priest said to Shaphan the scribe, "I have found the Book of the Law in the house of the Lord." And Hilkiah gave the book to Shaphan, and he read it. So Shaphan the scribe went to the king, bringing the king word, saying, "Your servants have gathered the money that was found in the house, and have delivered it into the hand of those who do the work, who oversee the house of the Lord"* (2 Kings 22:8-10 NKJV).

### *Reflections*

1. What did Shaphan the scribe read that changed King Josiah?

   _____

   _____

   _____

   _____

2. Where in the Bible is the 100-year-old prophecy of Josiah located?

_____

_____

_____

_____

# Decrees for Removing Every Evil Veil

And say, "Thus says the Lord God, 'Woe to the women who sew magic bands on all wrists and make veils for the heads of persons of every stature to hunt down lives! Will you hunt down the lives of My people, but preserve the lives of others for yourselves?'" (Ezekiel 13:18 NKJV)

## Prayer of Activation

### 1. Worship God

Heavenly Father, holy is Your name and greatly to be praised. You are the Father of Light and in You is no shadow of turning. I worship and adore You in Yeshua's name, for this purpose was I created, to give You pleasure through my love and adoration. May Your Kingdom manifest in my life as it is in Heaven. Plead my cause, O Lord, with those who strive with me; fight against any entity or person who is contending against me and what is written about me in Your book of destiny. Heavenly Father, it is written in Psalm 27:6 (NASB), *"And now my head will be lifted up above my enemies around me, and I will offer sacrifices in His tent with shouts of joy; I will sing, yes, I will sing praises to the Lord."* Heavenly Father, I thank you that I will never be swallowed by the demonic powers because You are the Lifter of my head. Abba Father, I enjoin my worship to the heavenly chorus of worship of Your holy angels and the crowd of witnesses, in Yeshua's mighty name.

## 2. Enter the Courts of Heaven

Heavenly Father, Righteous Judge, I ask that the courts of Heaven be seated according to Daniel 7:9-10 (AMP) and that all books related to my life and destiny be opened. I ask this in Yeshua's mighty name. It is written: *"I kept looking until thrones were set up, and the Ancient of Days (God) took His seat; His garment was white as snow and the hair of His head like pure wool. His throne was flames of fire; its wheels were a burning fire. A river of fire was flowing and coming out from before Him; a thousand thousands were attending Him, and ten thousand times ten thousand were standing before Him; the court was seated, and the books were opened."* Heavenly Father, Righteous Judge, I am requesting the privilege of standing before the courtroom of the Ancient of Days according to what was revealed to the prophet Daniel, in Yeshua's name, I pray. Heavenly Father, I stand in Your royal courtroom because of the shed blood and finished work of Yeshua on the Cross. I have come to receive Your righteous judgment over my life against every evil veil that satan has been using against me. Heavenly Father, I call upon Your holy angels to be witnesses to my lawsuit and righteous prosecution of every evil veil that is working against me. I decree and declare that every evil veil covering my spirit, soul, and body will be removed so I can achieve my God-given destiny here on earth, in Yeshua's name I pray.

## 3. Repent

Heavenly Father, Righteous Judge, it is written, *"If we confess our sins, He is faithful and just to forgive us our sins and to cleanse us from all unrighteousness"* (1 John 1:9 NKJV). I therefore activate the law of repentance and present before this court my heartfelt repentance for my personal transgressions, and for the iniquities of my forefathers who opened the door for every veil of darkness to oppress my life and bloodline, in Yeshua's name I pray. Heavenly Father, I ask that the blood of Yeshua wash away every iniquity of my forefathers that the enemy is using as a legal right to build cases against me and to bind me to every evil veil of darkness. I also repent for all self-inflicted word curses and covenants with demons that have existed in my ancestral bloodline. I am asking that every ancestral agreement with demonic powers and evil altars will now be revoked. I petition the courts of Heaven to silence their right to claim me and my bloodline, in Yeshua's name. Thank You, Lord, for revoking these demonically engineered covenants and evil altars in Yeshua's mighty name! Heavenly Father and Righteous Judge, it is my heartfelt desire to divorce myself from every evil veil of darkness that is operating in my life. I petition the Ancient of Days to grant me a verdict of judicial emancipation from the oppressive power of every evil veil of darkness. I receive Your favorable verdict by faith in Messiah's finished work and shed blood.

## 4. Petition the Courts of Heaven to Dismiss All of Satan's Charges

Heavenly Father and Righteous Judge, based upon Yeshua's finished work and my heartfelt repentance, I now move on the court of Heaven to dismiss all of satan's accusations and charges against me and my bloodline in Jesus's name. Righteous Judge, dismiss every one of satan's accusations connected to every evil veil that is oppressing my life. For it is written in Revelation 12:10 that the accuser of the brethren has been cast down. So I petition You, heavenly Father and Righteous Judge, to cast down all of satan's accusations against me and dismiss all of satan's charges against me, in Yeshua's name I pray.

## 5. Declare Your Authority in Christ

Heavenly Father and Righteous Judge, in Luke 10:19 (NKJV), Yeshua says, *"Behold, I give you the authority to trample on serpents and scorpions, and over all the power of the enemy, and nothing shall by any means hurt you."* Heavenly Father, as I prepare myself to pronounce powerful apostolic and prophetic decrees, I totally acknowledge my God-given authority in Christ to trample on serpents and scorpions that satan has weaponized against me and my destiny, in Yeshua's mighty name, I pray. The Bible also says in Proverbs 28:1 (NKJV), "*The wicked flee when no one pursues, but the righteous are bold as a lion.*" Heavenly Father, because of my God-given authority in Christ, I am as bold as lion. No messenger of satan, human or demonic, can intimidate me. I am like Mount Zion, which cannot be moved, in Yeshua's mighty name, I pray. I thank You, Heavenly Father, that in Mark 16:17-18, Yeshua gave me the authority to cast out devils and take up serpents and to bring God's healing power to those who are sick and oppressed. I therefore make the following decrees, completely assured of both my identity and authority in Christ Jesus!

## 6. Loudly Declare These Supernatural Decrees So You Can Have Your Breakthrough:

- Heavenly Father, I decree and declare that the power of every evil veil of darkness is completely broken over my life. I decree that I am no longer a victim of these demonic veils of darkness, in Yeshua's name.

- I decree and declare that You are setting me free from every evil spiritual veil that causes physical and spiritual deafness in Yeshua's name.

- I decree and declare that the Holy Spirit is setting me free from any veil of witchcraft or magic that has caused any kind of spiritual blindness in my life, in Yeshua's name, I pray.

- I decree and declare that the Holy Spirit is setting me free from every veil of deception that would cause me not to walk in the truthfulness of God's Word, in Yeshua's name, I pray.

- I decree and declare that as I bring my sacrificial offering into the courts of Heaven, the power of every evil veil that satan placed over my finances is now destroyed, in Yeshua's name.

- I decree and declare that every evil veil of darkness covering my mind and stopping my spiritual and mental transformation according to Romans 12:1 is removed in Yeshua's mighty name!

- I decree and declare that God is setting me free from every evil veil, which has caused me to be spiritually crippled in Yeshua's name, I pray.

- I decree and declare that everything, which has been stolen from my life because of evil veils of darkness, will now be restored back to me, in Yeshua's name, I pray.

## 7. End with Thanksgiving

Heavenly Father and Righteous Judge, I thank You that the foundation of Your throne is righteousness and justice. Thank You for giving me justice against the demonic entities behind these evil veils of darkness. Heavenly Father, I thank You that because of the finished work of Yeshua on the Cross, You have translated me from the kingdom of darkness to Your glorious Kingdom of Light! Heavenly Father, since You have adopted me into Your divine family, I thank You that You always hear me when I pray. I thank You that every apostolic and prophetic decree that I have made has been heard. Thank You, Lord, that everything I have just decreed is on its way to full manifestation in Yeshua's mighty name. Heavenly Father, until the manifestation, I will maintain an aggressive attitude of thanksgiving for the complete manifestation of what I have decreed today! In Yeshua's name I pray.

# Decrees for Overthrowing Witchcraft

For there is no sorcery against Jacob, nor any divination against Israel. It now must be said of Jacob and of Israel, "Oh, what God has done!" (**Numbers 23:23 NKJV**)

## Prayer of Activation

### 1. Worship God

Heavenly Father, holy is Your name and greatly to be praised. You are the Father of Light and in You is no shadow of turning. I worship and adore You in Yeshua's name, for this purpose was I created, to give You pleasure through my love and adoration. May Your Kingdom manifest in my life as it is in Heaven. Plead my cause, O Lord, with those who strive with me; fight against any entity or person who is contending against me and what is written about me in Your book of destiny. Heavenly Father, it is written in Psalm 27:6 (NASB), *"And now my head will be lifted above my enemies, around me, and I will offer sacrifices in His tent with shouts of joy; I will sing, yes, I will sing praises to the Lord."* Heavenly Father, I thank You that I will never be swallowed by the demonic powers because You are the Lifter of my head. Abba Father, I enjoin my worship to the heavenly chorus of worship of Your holy angels and the crowd of witnesses, in Yeshua's mighty name.

## 2. Enter the Courts of Heaven

Heavenly Father, Righteous Judge, I ask that the courts of Heaven be seated according to Daniel 7:9-10 (AMP) and that all books related to my life and destiny be opened. I ask this in Yeshua's mighty name. It is written: *"I kept looking until thrones were set up, and the Ancient of Days (God) took His seat; His garment was white as snow and the hair of His head like pure wool. His throne was flames of fire; its wheels were a burning fire. A river of fire was flowing and coming out from before Him; a thousand thousands were attending Him, and ten thousand times ten thousand were standing before Him; the court was seated, and the books were opened."* Heavenly Father, Righteous Judge, I am requesting the privilege of standing before the courtroom of the Ancient of Days according to what was revealed to the prophet Daniel, in Yeshua's name, I pray. Heavenly Father, I stand in Your royal courtroom because of the shed blood and finished work of Yeshua on the Cross. I have come to receive Your righteous judgment over my life against every form of witchcraft that satan has been using against me. Heavenly Father, I call upon Your holy angels to be witnesses to my lawsuit and righteous prosecution of every form of witchcraft that is working against me. I decree and declare that every form of witchcraft covering my spirit, soul, and body will be removed so I can achieve my God-given destiny here on earth, in Yeshua's name I pray.

## 3. Repent

Heavenly Father, Righteous Judge, it is written, *"If we confess our sins, He is faithful and just to forgive us our sins and to cleanse us from all unrighteousness"* (1 John 1:9 NKVJ). I therefore activate the law of repentance and present before this court my heartfelt repentance for my personal transgressions, and for the iniquities of my forefathers that opened the door for every form of witchcraft to oppress my life and bloodline, in Yeshua's name I pray. Heavenly Father, I ask that the blood of Yeshua wash away every iniquity of my forefathers that the enemy is using as a legal right to build cases against me and to bind me to every form of witchcraft. I also repent for all self-inflicted word curses and covenants with demons that have existed in my ancestral bloodline. I am asking that every ancestral agreement with demonic powers and evil altars will now be revoked. I petition the courts of Heaven to silence their right to claim me and my bloodline, in Yeshua's name. Thank You, Lord, for revoking these demonically engineered covenants and evil altars in Yeshua's mighty name! Heavenly Father and Righteous Judge, it is my heartfelt desire to divorce myself from every form of witchcraft that is operating in my life. I petition the Ancient of Days to grant me a verdict of judicial emancipation from the oppressive power of every form of witchcraft. I receive Your favorable verdict by faith in Messiah's finished work and shed blood.

## 4. Petition the Courts of Heaven to Dismiss All of Satan's Charges

Heavenly Father and Righteous Judge, based upon Yeshua's finished work and my heartfelt repentance, I now move on the Court of Heaven to dismiss all of satan's accusations and charges against me and my bloodline in Jesus's name. Righteous Judge, dismiss every one of satan's accusation connected to every form of witchcraft that is oppressing my life. For it is written in Revelation 12:10 that the accuser of the brethren has been cast down. So, I petition You, heavenly Father and Righteous Judge, to cast down all of satan's accusations against me and dismiss all of satan's charges against me, in Yeshua's name, I pray.

## 5. Declare Your Authority in Christ

Heavenly Father and Righteous Judge, in Luke 10:19 (NKJV), Yeshua said, *"Behold, I give you the authority to trample on serpents and scorpions, and over all the power of the enemy, and nothing shall by any means hurt you."* Heavenly Father, as I prepare myself to pronounce powerful apostolic and prophetic decrees, I totally acknowledge my God-given authority in Christ to trample on serpents and scorpions that satan has weaponized against me and my destiny, in Yeshua's mighty name, I pray. The Bible also says in Proverbs 28:1 (NKJV), "*The wicked flee when no one pursues, but the righteous are bold as a lion.*" Heavenly Father, because of my God-given authority in Christ, I am as bold as lion. No messenger of satan, human or demonic, can intimidate me. I am like Mount Zion, which cannot be moved, in Yeshua's mighty name, I pray. I thank You, heavenly Father, that in Mark 16:17-18, Yeshua gave me the authority to cast out devils and take up serpents and to bring God's healing power to those who are sick and oppressed. I therefore make the following decrees, completely assured of both my identity and authority in Christ Jesus!

## 6. Loudly Declare These Supernatural Decrees So You Can Have Your Breakthrough:

- Heavenly Father, I decree and declare that the power of every form of witchcraft is completely broken over my life. I decree that I am no longer a victim of every form of witchcraft, in Yeshua's name.

- I decree and declare that You are setting me free from every form of witchcraft that causes physical and spiritual deafness in Yeshua's name.

- I decree and declare that the Holy Spirit is setting me free from any veil of witchcraft or magic that has caused any kind of spiritual blindness in my life, in Yeshua's name, I pray.

- I decree and declare that the Holy Spirit is setting me free from every form of witchcraft that would cause me not to walk in the truthfulness of God's Word, in Yeshua's name, I pray.

- I decree and declare that as I bring my sacrificial offering into the courts of Heaven, the power of every form of witchcraft that satan placed over my finances is now destroyed, in Yeshua's name.

- I decree and declare that every form of witchcraft covering my mind and stopping my spiritual and mental transformation according to Romans 12:1 is removed in Yeshua's mighty name!

- I decree and declare that God is setting me free from every form of witchcraft, which has caused me to be spiritually crippled in Yeshua's name, I pray.

- I decree and declare that everything, which has been stolen from my life because any form of witchcraft, will now be restored back to me, in Yeshua's name, I pray.

## 7. End with Thanksgiving

Heavenly Father and Righteous Judge, I thank You that the foundation of Your throne is righteousness and justice. Thank You for giving me justice against the demonic entities behind every form of witchcraft that is fighting me. Heavenly Father, I thank You that because of the finished work of Yeshua on the Cross, You have translated me from the kingdom of darkness to Your glorious Kingdom of Light! Heavenly Father, since You have adopted me into Your divine family, I thank You that You always hear me, when I pray. I thank You that every apostolic and prophetic decree that I have made has been heard. Thank You, Lord, that everything I have just decreed is on its way to full manifestation in Yeshua's mighty name. Heavenly Father, until the manifestation, I will maintain an aggressive attitude of thanksgiving for the complete manifestation of what I have decreed today! In Yeshua's name I pray.

# Decrees for Destroying
# Evil Foundations

In his days Hiel the Bethelite built Jericho; he laid its foundations with the loss of Abiram his firstborn and set up its gates with
the loss of his youngest son Segub, according to the word of the
Lord, which He spoke by Joshua the son of Nun (**1 Kings 16:34
NASB1995**).

## Prayer of Activation

### *1. Worship God*

Heavenly Father, holy is Your name and greatly to be praised. You are
the Father of Light and in You is no shadow of turning. I worship
and adore You in Yeshua's name, for this purpose was I created,
to give You pleasure through my love and adoration. May Your Kingdom
manifest in my life as it is in Heaven. Plead my cause, O Lord, with those
who strive with me; fight against any entity or person who is contending
against me and what is written about me in Your book of destiny. Heavenly
Father, it is written in Psalm 27:6 (NASB), *"And now my head will be lifted
above my enemies around me, and I will offer sacrifices in His tent with shouts*

*of joy; I will sing, yes, I will sing praises to the Lord."* Heavenly Father, I thank You that I will never be swallowed by the demonic powers because You are the Lifter of my head. Abba Father, I enjoin my worship to the heavenly chorus of worship of Your holy angels and the crowd of witnesses, in Yeshua's mighty name.

## 2. Enter the Courts of Heaven

Heavenly Father, Righteous Judge, I ask that the courts of Heaven be seated according to Daniel 7:9-10 (AMP) and that all books related to my life and destiny be opened. I ask this in Yeshua's mighty name. It is written: *"I kept looking until thrones were set up, and the Ancient of Days (God) took His seat; His garment was white as snow and the hair of His head like pure wool. His throne was flames of fire; its wheels were a burning fire. A river of fire was flowing and coming out from before Him; a thousand thousands were attending Him, and ten thousand times ten thousand were standing before Him; the court was seated, and the books were opened."* Heavenly Father, Righteous Judge, I am requesting the privilege of standing before the courtroom of the Ancient of Days according to what was revealed to the prophet Daniel, in Yeshua's name, I pray. Heavenly Father, I stand in Your royal courtroom because of the shed blood and finished work of Yeshua on the Cross. I have come to receive Your righteous judgment over my life against every evil foundation that satan has been using against me. Heavenly Father, I call upon Your holy angels to be witnesses to my lawsuit and righteous prosecution of every evil foundation that is working against me. I decree and declare that every evil foundation covering my spirit, soul, and body will be removed so I can achieve my God-given destiny here on earth, in Yeshua's name I pray.

## 3. Repent

Heavenly Father, Righteous Judge, it is written, *"If we confess our sins, He is faithful and just to forgive us our sins and to cleanse us from all unrighteousness"*

(1 John 1:9 NKJV). I therefore activate the law of repentance and present before this court my heartfelt repentance for my personal transgressions, and for the iniquities of my forefathers that opened the door for every veil of darkness to oppress my life and bloodline, in Yeshua's name I pray. Heavenly Father, I ask that the blood of Yeshua wash away every iniquity of my forefathers that the enemy is using as a legal right to build cases against me and to bind me to every evil foundation. I also repent for all self-inflicted word curses and covenants with demons that have existed in my ancestral bloodline. I am asking that every ancestral agreement with demonic powers and evil altars will now be revoked. I petition the courts of Heaven to silence their right to claim me and my bloodline, in Yeshua's name. Thank You, Lord, for revoking these demonically engineered covenants and evil altars in Yeshua's mighty name! Heavenly Father and Righteous Judge, it is my heartfelt desire to divorce myself from every evil foundation that is operating in my life. I petition the Ancient of Days to grant me a verdict of judicial emancipation from the oppressive power of every evil foundation. I receive your favorable verdict by faith in Messiah's finished work and shed blood.

### 4. Petition the Courts of Heaven to Dismiss All of Satan's Charges

Heavenly Father and Righteous Judge, based upon Yeshua's finished work and my heartfelt repentance, I now move on the court of Heaven to dismiss all of satan's accusations and charges against me and my bloodline in Jesus's name. Righteous Judge, dismiss every one of satan's accusation connected to every evil foundation that is oppressing my life. For it is written in Revelation 12:10 that the accuser of the brethren has been cast down. So, I petition You, heavenly Father and Righteous Judge, to cast down all of satan's accusations against me and dismiss all of satan's charges against me, in Yeshua's name, I pray.

## 5. Declare Your Authority in Christ

Heavenly Father and Righteous Judge, in Luke 10:19 (NKJV), Yeshua said, *"Behold, I give you the authority to trample on serpents and scorpions, and over all the power of the enemy, and nothing shall by any means hurt you."* Heavenly Father, as I prepare myself to pronounce powerful apostolic and prophetic decrees, I totally acknowledge my God-given authority in Christ to trample on serpents and scorpions that Satan has weaponized against me and my destiny, in Yeshua's mighty name, I pray. The Bible also says in Proverbs 28:1 (NKJV), *"The wicked flee when no one pursues, but the righteous are bold as a lion."* Heavenly Father, because of my God-given authority in Christ, I am as bold as lion. No messenger of satan, human or demonic, can intimidate me. I am like Mount Zion, which cannot be moved, in Yeshua's mighty name, I pray. I thank You, heavenly Father, that in Mark 16:17-18, Yeshua gave me the authority to cast out devils and take up serpents and to bring God's healing power to those who are sick and oppressed. I therefore make the following decrees, completely assured of both my identity and authority in Christ Jesus!

## 6. Loudly Declare These Supernatural Decrees So You Can Have Your Breakthrough:

- Heavenly Father I decree and declare that the power of every evil foundation of darkness is completely broken over my life. I decree that I am no longer a victim of these evil foundations of darkness, in Yeshua's name.

- I decree and declare that You are setting me free from every evil foundation that causes physical and spiritual deafness in Yeshua's name.

- I decree and declare that the Holy Spirit is setting me free from every evil foundation of witchcraft or magic that has caused any kind of spiritual blindness in my life, in Yeshua's name, I pray.

- I decree and declare that the Holy Spirit is setting me free from every evil foundation that would cause me not to walk in the truthfulness of God's Word, in Yeshua's name, I pray.

- I decree and declare that as I bring my sacrificial offering into the courts of Heaven, the power of every evil foundation that satan placed over my finances is now destroyed, in Yeshua's name.

- I decree and declare that every evil foundation covering my mind and stopping my spiritual and mental transformation according to Romans 12:1 is removed in Yeshua's mighty name!

- I decree and declare that God is setting me free from every evil foundation, which has caused me to be spiritually crippled in Yeshua's name, I pray.

- I decree and declare that everything, which has been stolen from my life because of evil foundations, will now be restored back to me, in Yeshua's name, I pray.

## 7. End with Thanksgiving

Heavenly Father and Righteous Judge, I thank You that the foundation of Your throne is righteousness and justice. Thank You for giving me justice against the demonic entities behind every evil foundation in my life. Heavenly Father, I thank You that because of the finished work of Yeshua on the

Cross, You have translated me from the kingdom of darkness to Your glorious Kingdom of Light! Heavenly Father, since You have adopted me into Your divine family, I thank You that always hear me, when I pray. I thank You that every apostolic and prophetic decree that I have made has been heard. Thank You, Lord, that everything I have just decreed is on its way to full manifestation in Yeshua's mighty name. Heavenly Father, until the manifestation, I will maintain an aggressive attitude of thanksgiving for the complete manifestation of what I have decreed today! In Yeshua's name I pray.

# Decrees for Arresting Blocking Spirits

Then he said to me, "Do not fear, Daniel, for from the first day that you set your heart to understand, and to humble yourself before your God, your words were heard; and I have come because of your words. But the prince of the kingdom of Persia withstood me twenty-one days; and behold, Michael, one of the chief princes, came to help me, for I had been left alone there with the kings of Persia" (Daniel 10:12-13 NKJV).

## Prayer of Activation

### 1. Worship God

Heavenly Father, holy is Your name and greatly to be praised. You are the Father of Light and in You is no shadow of turning. I worship and adore You in Yeshua's name, for this purpose was I created, to give You pleasure through my love and adoration. May Your Kingdom manifest in my life as it is in Heaven. Plead my cause, O Lord, with those who strive with me; fight against any entity or person who is contending against me and what is written about me in Your book of destiny. Heavenly Father, it is written in Psalm 27:6 (NASB), *"And now my head will be lifted up above my enemies around me, and I will offer sacrifices in His tent with shouts of joy;*

*I will sing, yes, I will sing praises to the Lord."* Heavenly Father, I thank You that I will never be swallowed by the demonic powers because You are the Lifter of my head. Abba Father, I enjoin my worship to the heavenly chorus of worship of Your holy angels and the crowd of witnesses, in Yeshua's mighty name.

## 2. Enter the Courts of Heaven

Heavenly Father, Righteous Judge, I ask that the courts of Heaven be seated according to Daniel 7:9-10 (AMP) and that all books related to my life and destiny be opened. I ask this in Yeshua's mighty name. It is written: *"I kept looking until thrones were set up, and the Ancient of Days (God) took His seat; His garment was white as snow and the hair of His head like pure wool. His throne was flames of fire; its wheels were a burning fire. A river of fire was flowing and coming out from before Him; a thousand thousands were attending Him, and ten thousand times ten thousand were standing before Him; the court was seated, and the books were opened."* Heavenly Father, Righteous Judge, I am requesting the privilege of standing before the courtroom of the Ancient of Days according to what was revealed to the prophet Daniel, in Yeshua's name, I pray. Heavenly Father, I stand in Your royal courtroom because of the shed blood and finished work of Yeshua on the Cross. I have come to receive Your righteous judgment over my life against every blocking spirit that satan has been using against me. Heavenly Father, I call upon Your holy angels to be witnesses to my lawsuit and righteous prosecution of every blocking spirit that is working against me. I decree and declare that every blocking spirit covering my spirit, soul, and body will be removed so I can achieve my God-given destiny here on earth, in Yeshua's name I pray.

## 3. Repent

Heavenly Father, Righteous Judge, it is written, *"If we confess our sins, He is faithful and just to forgive us our sins and to cleanse us from all unrighteousness"*

(1 John 1:9 NKJV). I therefore activate the law of repentance and present before this court my heartfelt repentance for my personal transgressions, and for the iniquities of my forefathers that opened the door for every blocking spirit to oppress my life and bloodline, in Yeshua's name I pray. Heavenly Father, I ask that the blood of Yeshua wash away every iniquity of my forefathers that the enemy is using as a legal right to build cases against me and to bind me to every blocking spirit. I also repent for all self-inflicted word curses and covenants with demons that have existed in my ancestral bloodline. I am asking that every ancestral agreement with demonic powers and evil altars will now be revoked. I petition the courts of Heaven to silence their right to claim me and my bloodline, in Yeshua's name. Thank You, Lord, for revoking these demonically engineered covenants and evil altars in Yeshua's mighty name! Heavenly Father and Righteous Judge, it is my heartfelt desire to divorce myself from every blocking spirit that is operating in my life. I petition the Ancient of Days to grant me a verdict of judicial emancipation from the oppressive power of every blocking spirit. I receive Your favorable verdict by faith in Messiah's finished work and shed blood.

## 4. Petition the Courts of Heaven to Dismiss All of Satan's Charges

Heavenly Father and Righteous Judge, based upon Yeshua's finished work and my heartfelt repentance, I now move on the court of Heaven to dismiss all of satan's accusations and charges against me and my bloodline in Jesus's name. Righteous Judge, dismiss every one of satan's accusation connected to every blocking spirit that is oppressing my life. For it is written in Revelation 12:10 that the accuser of the brethren has been cast down. So, I petition You, heavenly Father and Righteous Judge, to cast down all of satan's accusations against me and dismiss all of satan's charges against me, in Yeshua's name, I pray.

## 5. Declare Your Authority in Christ

Heavenly Father and Righteous Judge, in Luke 10:19 (NKJV), Yeshua says, *"Behold, I give you the authority to trample on serpents and scorpions, and over all the power of the enemy, and nothing shall by any means hurt you."* Heavenly Father as I prepare myself to pronounce powerful apostolic and prophetic decrees, I totally acknowledge my God-given authority in Christ to trample on serpents and scorpions that satan has weaponized against me and my destiny, in Yeshua's mighty name, I pray. The Bible also says in Proverbs 28:1 (NKJV), *"The wicked flee when no one pursues, but the righteous are bold as a lion."* Heavenly Father because of my God-given authority in Christ, I am as bold as lion. No messenger of satan, human or demonic, can intimidate me. I am like Mount Zion, which cannot be moved, in Yeshua's mighty name, I pray. I thank You, heavenly Father, that in Mark 16:17-18, Yeshua gave me the authority to cast out devils and take up serpents and to bring God's healing power to those who are sick and oppressed. I therefore make the following decrees, completely assured of both my identity and authority in Christ Jesus!

## 6. Loudly Declare These Supernatural Decrees So You Can Have Your Breakthrough:

- Heavenly Father, I decree and declare that the power of every blocking spirit of darkness is completely broken over my life. I decree that I am no longer a victim of these blocking spirits, in Yeshua's name.

- I decree and declare that You are setting me free from every blocking spirit that causes physical and spiritual deafness in Yeshua's name.

- I decree and declare that the Holy Spirit is setting me free from any blocking spirit of witchcraft or magic that has caused any kind of spiritual blindness in my life, in Yeshua's name, I pray.

- I decree and declare that the Holy Spirit is setting me free from every blocking spirit that would cause me not to walk in the truthfulness of God's Word, in Yeshua's name, I pray.

- I decree and declare that as I bring my sacrificial offering into the Courts of Heaven, the power of every blocking spirit that satan placed over my finances is now destroyed, in Yeshua's name.

- I decree and declare that every blocking spirit covering my mind and stopping my spiritual and mental transformation according to Romans 12:1 is removed in Yeshua's mighty name!

- I decree and declare that God is setting me free from every blocking spirit, which has caused me to be spiritually crippled in Yeshua's name, I pray.

- I decree and declare that everything, which has been stolen from my life because of these blocking spirits, will now be restored back to me, in Yeshua's name, I pray.

## 7. End with Thanksgiving

Heavenly Father and Righteous Judge, I thank You that the foundation of Your throne is righteousness and justice. Thank You for giving me justice against the demonic entities behind these blocking spirits. Heavenly Father, I thank You that because of the finished work of Yeshua on the Cross, You have translated me from the kingdom of darkness to Your glorious Kingdom of Light! Heavenly Father, since You have adopted me into Your divine family, I thank You that You always hear me, when I pray. I thank You that every apostolic and prophetic decree that I have made has been heard. Thank You, Lord, that everything I have just decreed is on its way to full manifestation in Yeshua's mighty name. Heavenly Father, until the manifestation, I will maintain an aggressive attitude of thanksgiving for the complete manifestation of what I have decreed today! In Yeshua's name I pray.

# Decrees for Silencing Evil Winds

While he was still speaking, another also came and said, "Your sons and daughters were eating and drinking wine in their oldest brother's house, and suddenly a great wind came from across the wilderness and struck the four corners of the house, and it fell on the young people, and they are dead; and I alone have escaped to tell you!" (**Job 1:18-19 NKJV**)

## Prayer of Activation

### 1. Worship God

Heavenly Father, holy is Your name and greatly to be praised. You are the Father of Light and in You is no shadow of turning. I worship and adore You in Yeshua's name, for this purpose was I created, to give You pleasure through my love and adoration. May Your Kingdom manifest in my life as it is in Heaven. Plead my cause, O Lord, with those who strive with me; fight against any entity or person who is contending against me and what is written about me in Your book of destiny. Heavenly Father, it is written in Psalm 27:6 (NASB), *"And now my head will be lifted up above my enemies around me, and I will offer sacrifices in His tent with shouts of joy; I will sing, yes, I will sing praises to the Lord."* Heavenly Father, I thank You

that I will never be swallowed by the demonic powers because You are the Lifter of my head. Abba Father, I enjoin my worship to the heavenly chorus of worship of Your holy angels and the crowd of witnesses, in Yeshua's mighty name.

## 2. Enter the Courts of Heaven

Heavenly Father, Righteous Judge, I ask that the courts of Heaven be seated according to Daniel 7:9-10 (AMP) and that all books related to my life and destiny be opened. I ask this in Yeshua's mighty name. It is written: *"I kept looking until thrones were set up, and the Ancient of Days (God) took His seat; His garment was white as snow and the hair of His head like pure wool. His throne was flames of fire; its wheels were a burning fire. A river of fire was flowing and coming out from before Him; a thousand thousands were attending Him, and ten thousand times ten thousand were standing before Him; the court was seated, and the books were opened."* Heavenly Father, Righteous Judge, I am requesting the privilege of standing before the courtroom of the Ancient of Days according to what was revealed to the prophet Daniel, in Yeshua's name, I pray. Heavenly Father, I stand in Your royal courtroom because of the shed blood and finished work of Yeshua on the Cross. I have come to receive Your righteous judgment over my life against every evil wind that satan has been using against me. Heavenly Father, I call upon Your holy angels to be witnesses to my lawsuit and righteous prosecution of every evil wind that is working against me. I decree and declare that every evil wind covering my spirit, soul, and body will be removed so I can achieve my God-given destiny here on earth, in Yeshua's name I pray.

## 3. Repent

Heavenly Father, Righteous Judge, it is written, *"If we confess our sins, He is faithful and just to forgive us our sins and to cleanse us from all unrighteousness"* (1 John 1:9 NKJV). I therefore activate the law of repentance and present

before this court my heartfelt repentance for my personal transgressions, and for the iniquities of my forefathers that opened the door for every evil wind to oppress my life and bloodline, in Yeshua's name I pray. Heavenly Father, I ask that the blood of Yeshua wash away every iniquity of my forefathers that the enemy is using as a legal right to build cases against me and to bind me to every evil wind. I also repent for all self-inflicted word curses and covenants with demons that have existed in my ancestral bloodline. I am asking that every ancestral agreement with demonic powers and evil altars will now be revoked. I petition the courts of Heaven to silence their right to claim me and my bloodline, in Yeshua's name. Thank You, Lord, for revoking these demonically engineered covenants and evil altars in Yeshua's mighty name! Heavenly Father and Righteous Judge, it is my heartfelt desire to divorce myself from every evil wind that is operating in my life. I petition the Ancient of Days to grant me a verdict of judicial emancipation from the oppressive power of every evil wind. I receive Your favorable verdict by faith in Messiah's finished work and shed blood.

## 4. Petition the Courts of Heaven to Dismiss All of Satan's Charges

Heavenly Father and Righteous Judge, based upon Yeshua's finished work and my heartfelt repentance, I now move on the court of Heaven to dismiss all of satan's accusations and charges against me and my bloodline in Jesus's name. Righteous Judge, dismiss every one of satan's accusation connected to every evil wind that is oppressing my life. For it is written in Revelation 12:10 that the accuser of the brethren has been cast down. So, I petition You, heavenly Father and Righteous Judge, to cast down all of satan's accusations against me and dismiss all of satan's charges against me, in Yeshua's name, I pray.

## 5. Declare Your Authority in Christ

Heavenly Father and Righteous Judge, in Luke 10:19 (NKJV), Yeshua says, *"Behold, I give you the authority to trample on serpents and scorpions, and over all the power of the enemy, and nothing shall by any means hurt you."* Heavenly Father, as I prepare myself to pronounce powerful apostolic and prophetic decrees, I totally acknowledge my God-given authority in Christ to trample on serpents and scorpions that Satan has weaponized against me and my destiny, in Yeshua's mighty name, I pray. The Bible also says in Proverbs 28:1 (NKJV), *"The wicked flee when no one pursues, but the righteous are bold as a lion."* Heavenly Father because of my God-given authority in Christ, I am as bold as lion. No messenger of satan, human or demonic, can intimidate me. I am like Mount Zion, which cannot be moved, in Yeshua's mighty name, I pray. I thank You, heavenly Father, that in Mark 16:17-18, Yeshua gave me the authority to cast out devils and take up serpents and to bring God's healing power to those who are sick and oppressed. I therefore make the following decrees, completely assured of both my identity and authority in Christ Jesus!

## 6. Loudly Declare These Supernatural Decrees So You Can Have Your Breakthrough:

- Heavenly Father, I decree and declare that the power of every evil wind of darkness is completely broken over my life. I decree that I am no longer a victim of these demonic evil winds, in Yeshua's name.

- I decree and declare that You are setting me free from every evil wind that causes physical and spiritual deafness, in Yeshua's name.

- I decree and declare that the Holy Spirit is setting me free from any evil wind of witchcraft or magic that has caused any kind of spiritual blindness in my life, in Yeshua's name, I pray.

- I decree and declare that the Holy Spirit is setting me free from every evil wind of deception that would cause me not to walk in the truthfulness of God's Word, in Yeshua's name, I pray.

- I decree and declare that as I bring my sacrificial offering into the courts of Heaven, the power of every evil wind that satan placed over my finances is now destroyed, in Yeshua's name.

- I decree and declare that every evil wind of darkness covering my mind and stopping my spiritual and mental transformation according to Romans 12:1 is removed in Yeshua's mighty name!

- I decree and declare that God is setting me free from every evil wind, which has caused me to be spiritually crippled in Yeshua's name, I pray.

- I decree and declare that everything, which has been stolen from my life because of every evil wind, will now be restored back to me, in Yeshua's name, I pray.

## 7. End with Thanksgiving

Heavenly Father and Righteous Judge, I thank You that the foundation of Your throne is righteousness and justice. Thank You for giving me justice against the demonic entities behind these evil winds. Heavenly Father, I thank You that because of the finished work of Yeshua on the Cross, You have translated me from the kingdom of darkness to Your glorious Kingdom of Light! Heavenly Father, since You have adopted me into Your divine family, I thank You that You always hear me, when I pray. I thank You that every apostolic and prophetic decree that I have made has been heard. Thank You, Lord, that everything I have just decreed is on its way to full manifestation in Yeshua's mighty name. Heavenly Father, until the manifestation, I will maintain an aggressive attitude of thanksgiving for the complete manifestation of what I have decreed today! In Yeshua's name I pray.

# Decrees for Establishing the Kingdom of God

So He said to them, "When you pray, say: Our Father in heaven, hallowed be Your name. Your kingdom come. Your will be done on earth as it is in heaven" (**Luke 11:2 NKJV**).

## Prayer of Activation

### 1. Worship God

Heavenly Father, holy is Your name and greatly to be praised. You are the Father of Light and in You is no shadow of turning. I worship and adore You in Yeshua's name, for this purpose was I created, to give You pleasure through my love and adoration. May Your Kingdom manifest in my life as it is in Heaven. Plead my cause, O Lord, with those who strive with me; fight against any entity or person who is contending against me and what is written about me in Your book of destiny. Heavenly Father, it is written in Psalm 27:6 (NASB), *"And now my head will be lifted up above my enemies around me, and I will offer sacrifices in His tent with shouts of joy; I will sing, yes, I will sing praises to the Lord."* Heavenly Father, I thank You that I will never be swallowed by the demonic powers because You are the

Lifter of my head. Abba Father, I enjoin my worship to the heavenly chorus of worship of Your holy angels and the crowd of witnesses, in Yeshua's mighty name.

## 2. Enter the Courts of Heaven

Heavenly Father, Righteous Judge, I ask that the courts of Heaven be seated according to Daniel 7:9-10 (AMP) and that all books related to my life and destiny be opened. I ask this in Yeshua's mighty name. It is written: *"I kept looking until thrones were set up, and the Ancient of Days (God) took His seat; His garment was white as snow and the hair of His head like pure wool. His throne was flames of fire; its wheels were a burning fire. A river of fire was flowing and coming out from before Him; a thousand thousands were attending Him, and ten thousand times ten thousand were standing before Him; the court was seated, and the books were opened."* Heavenly Father, Righteous Judge, I am requesting the privilege of standing before the courtroom of the Ancient of Days according to what was revealed to the prophet Daniel, in Yeshua's name, I pray. Heavenly Father, I stand in Your royal courtroom because of the shed blood and finished work of Yeshua on the Cross. I have come to receive Your righteous judgment over my life against every evil scheme that satan has been using against me to stop me from manifesting the Kingdom of God. Heavenly Father, I call upon Your holy angels to be witnesses to my lawsuit and righteous prosecution of every evil scheme that satan has been using against me to stop me from manifesting the Kingdom of God. I decree and declare that every evil veil covering my spirit, soul, and body will be removed so I can achieve my God-given destiny here on earth, in Yeshua's name I pray.

## 3. Repent

Heavenly Father, Righteous Judge, it is written, *"If we confess our sins, He is faithful and just to forgive us our sins and to cleanse us from all unrighteousness"* (1 John 1:9 NKJV). I therefore activate the law of repentance and present before this court my heartfelt repentance for my personal transgressions, and for the iniquities of my forefathers that opened the door for every evil scheme that satan has been using against me to stop me from manifesting the Kingdom of God, in Yeshua's name I pray. Heavenly Father, I ask that the blood of Yeshua wash away every iniquity of my forefathers that the enemy is using as a legal right to build cases against me and to stop me from manifesting the Kingdom of God. I also repent for all self-inflicted word curses and covenants with demons that have existed in my ancestral bloodline. I am asking that every ancestral agreement with demonic powers and evil altars will now be revoked. I petition the courts of Heaven to silence their right to claim me and my bloodline, in Yeshua's name. Thank You, Lord, for revoking these demonically engineered covenants and evil altars in Yeshua's mighty name! Heavenly Father and Righteous Judge, it is my heartfelt desire to divorce myself from every evil scheme that satan has been using against me to stop me from manifesting the Kingdom of God. I petition the Ancient of Days to grant me a verdict of judicial emancipation from the oppressive power of every evil scheme that satan has been using against me to stop me from manifesting the Kingdom of God. I receive Your favorable verdict by faith in Messiah's finished work and shed blood.

## 4. Petition the Courts of Heaven to Dismiss All of Satan's Charges

Heavenly Father and Righteous Judge, based upon Yeshua's finished work and my heartfelt repentance, I now move on the court of Heaven to dismiss all of satan's accusations and charges against me and my bloodline in Jesus's name. Righteous Judge, dismiss every evil scheme that satan has been using against me to stop me from manifesting the Kingdom of God. For it is written in Revelation 12:10 that the accuser of the brethren has been cast down. So, I petition You, heavenly Father and Righteous Judge, to cast down all of

satan's accusations against me and dismiss all of satan's charges against me, in Yeshua's name, I pray.

## 5. Declare Your Authority in Christ

Heavenly Father and Righteous Judge, in Luke 10:19 (NKJV), Yeshua says, *"Behold, I give you the authority to trample on serpents and scorpions, and over all the power of the enemy, and nothing shall by any means hurt you."* Heavenly Father as I prepare myself to pronounce powerful apostolic and prophetic decrees, I totally acknowledge my God-given authority in Christ to trample on serpents and scorpions that satan has weaponized against me and my destiny, in Yeshua's mighty name, I pray. The Bible also says in Proverbs 28:1 (NKJV), *"The wicked flee when no one pursues, but the righteous are bold as a lion."* Heavenly Father because of my God-given authority in Christ, I am as bold as lion. No messenger of satan, human or demonic, can intimidate me. I am like Mount Zion, which cannot be moved, in Yeshua's mighty name, I pray. I thank You, heavenly Father, that in Mark 16:17-18, Yeshua gave me the authority to cast out devils and take up serpents and to bring God's healing power to those who are sick and oppressed. I therefore make the following decrees, completely assured of both my identity and authority in Christ Jesus!

## 6. Loudly Declare These Supernatural Decrees So You Can Have Your Breakthrough:

- Heavenly Father, I decree and declare that the power of every evil scheme that satan has been using against me to stop me from manifesting the Kingdom of God is completely broken over my life. I decree that I am no longer a victim of these evil schemes that satan has been using to stop me from manifesting the Kingdom of God, in Yeshua's name.

- I decree and declare that You are setting me free from every evil scheme that satan has been using against me to stop me from manifesting the Kingdom of God for the healing of physical and spiritual deafness in Yeshua's name.

- I decree and declare that the Holy Spirit is setting me free from any evil scheme that satan has been using against me to stop me from manifesting the Kingdom of God, which has caused any kind of spiritual blindness in my life, in Yeshua's name, I pray.

- I decree and declare that the Holy Spirit is setting me free from every evil scheme that satan has been using against me to stop me from manifesting the Kingdom of God and cause me not to walk in the truthfulness of God's Word, in Yeshua's name, I pray.

- I decree and declare that as I bring my sacrificial offering into the courts of Heaven, the power of every evil scheme that satan has been using against me to stop me from manifesting Kingdom finances is now destroyed, in Yeshua's name.

- I decree and declare that every evil scheme that satan has been using against me to stop me from manifesting the Kingdom of God in the area of spiritual and mental transformation according to Romans 12:1 is now removed in Yeshua's mighty name!

- I decree and declare that God is setting me free from every evil scheme that satan has been using against me to stop me from manifesting the Kingdom of God, which has caused me to be spiritually crippled in Yeshua's name, I pray.

- I decree and declare that everything, which has been stolen from my life because of satan's evil schemes, will now be restored back to me, in Yeshua's name, I pray.

## 7. End with Thanksgiving

Heavenly Father and Righteous Judge, I thank You that the foundation of Your throne is righteousness and justice. Thank You for giving me justice against the demonic entities behind every evil scheme that satan has been using against me to stop me from manifesting the Kingdom of God. Heavenly Father, I thank You that because of the finished work of Yeshua on the Cross, You have translated me from the kingdom of darkness to Your glorious Kingdom of Light! Heavenly Father, since You have adopted me into Your divine family, I thank You that You always hear me, when I pray. I thank You that every apostolic and prophetic decree that I have made has been heard. Thank You, Lord, that everything I have just decreed is on its way to full manifestation in Yeshua's mighty name. Heavenly Father, until the manifestation, I will maintain an aggressive attitude of thanksgiving for the complete manifestation of what I have decreed today! In Yeshua's name I pray.

# Decrees for Silencing the Python Spirit

One day, as we were going to the house of prayer, we encountered a young slave girl who had an evil spirit of divination, the spirit of Python. She had earned great profits for her owners by being a fortune-teller. She kept following us, shouting, "These men are servants of the Great High God, and they're telling us how to be saved!" Day after day she continued to do this, until Paul, greatly annoyed, turned and said to the spirit indwelling her, "I command you in the name of Jesus, the Anointed One, to come out of her, now!" At that very moment, the spirit came out of her! (**Acts 16:16-18 The Passion Translation**)

## Prayer of Activation

### 1. Worship God

Heavenly Father, holy is Your name and greatly to be praised. You are the Father of Light and in You is no shadow of turning. I worship and adore You in Yeshua's name, for this purpose was I created, to give You pleasure through my love and adoration. May Your Kingdom manifest in my life as it is in Heaven. Plead my cause, O Lord, with those who strive with me; fight against any entity or person who is contending against me and what is written about me in Your book of destiny. Heavenly Father, it is written in Psalm 27:6 (NASB), *"And now my head will be lifted up above my enemies around me, and I will offer sacrifices in His tent with shouts of joy; I will sing, yes, I will sing praises to the Lord."* Heavenly Father, I thank You that I will never be swallowed by the demonic powers because You are the Lifter of my head. Abba Father, I enjoin my worship to the heavenly chorus of worship of Your holy angels and the crowd of witnesses, in Yeshua's mighty name.

## 2. Enter the Courts of Heaven

Heavenly Father, Righteous Judge, I ask that the Courts of Heaven be seated according to Daniel 7:9-10 (AMP) and that all books related to my life and destiny be opened. I ask this in Yeshua's mighty name. It is written: *"I kept looking until thrones were set up, and the Ancient of Days (God) took His seat; His garment was white as snow and the hair of His head like pure wool. His throne was flames of fire; its wheels were a burning fire. A river of fire was flowing and coming out from before Him; a thousand thousands were attending Him, and ten thousand times ten thousand were standing before Him; the court was seated, and the books were opened."* Heavenly Father, Righteous Judge, I am requesting the privilege of standing before the courtroom of the Ancient of Days according to what was revealed to the prophet Daniel, in Yeshua's name, I pray. Heavenly Father, I stand in Your royal courtroom because of the shed blood and finished work of Yeshua on the Cross. I have come to receive Your righteous judgment over my life against silencing the python spirit that satan has been using against me. Heavenly Father, I call upon Your holy angels to be witnesses to my lawsuit and righteous prosecution of every python spirit that is working against me. I decree and declare that every python spirit covering my spirit, soul, and body will be removed so I can achieve my God-given destiny here on earth, in Yeshua's name I pray.

## 3. Repent

Heavenly Father, Righteous Judge, it is written, *"If we confess our sins, He is faithful and just to forgive us our sins and to cleanse us from all unrighteousness"* (1 John 1:9 NKJV). I therefore activate the law of repentance and present before this court my heartfelt repentance for my personal transgressions, and for the iniquities of my forefathers that opened the door for the python spirit to oppress my life and bloodline, in Yeshua's name I pray. Heavenly Father, I ask that the blood of Yeshua wash away every iniquity of my forefathers that the enemy is using as a legal right to build cases against me and to bind me to the python spirit. I also repent for all self-inflicted word curses and covenants with demons that have existed in my ancestral bloodline. I am asking that every ancestral agreement with demonic powers and evil altars will now be revoked. I petition the courts of Heaven to silence their right to claim me and my bloodline, in Yeshua's name. Thank You, Lord, for revoking these demonically engineered covenants and evil altars in Yeshua's mighty name! Heavenly Father and Righteous Judge, it is my heartfelt desire to divorce myself from every python spirit that is operating in my life. I petition the Ancient of Days to grant me a verdict of judicial emancipation from the oppressive power of the python spirit. I receive Your favorable verdict by faith in Messiah's finished work and shed blood.

## 4. Petition the Courts of Heaven to Dismiss All of Satan's Charges

Heavenly Father and Righteous Judge, based upon Yeshua's finished work and my heartfelt repentance, I now move on the court of Heaven to dismiss all of satan's accusations and charges against me and my bloodline in Jesus's name. Righteous Judge, dismiss every one of satan's accusation connected to the python spirit that is oppressing my life. For it is written in Revelation 12:10 that the accuser of the brethren has been cast down. So, I petition You, heavenly Father and Righteous Judge to cast down all of satan's accusations against me and dismiss all of satan's charges against me, in Yeshua's name, I pray.

## 5. Declare Your Authority in Christ

Heavenly Father and Righteous Judge, in Luke 10:19 (NKJV), Yeshua says, *"Behold, I give you the authority to trample on serpents and scorpions, and over all the power of the enemy, and nothing shall by any means hurt you."* Heavenly Father, as I prepare myself to pronounce powerful apostolic and prophetic decrees, I totally acknowledge my God-given authority in Christ to trample on serpents and scorpions that satan has weaponized against me and my destiny, in Yeshua's mighty name, I pray. The Bible also says in Proverbs 28:1 (NKJV), *"The wicked flee when no one pursues, but the righteous are bold as a lion."* Heavenly Father, because of my God-given authority in Christ, I am as bold as lion. No messenger of satan, human or demonic, can intimidate me. I am like Mount Zion, which cannot be moved, in Yeshua's mighty name, I pray. I thank You, heavenly Father, that in Mark 16:17-18, Yeshua gave me the authority to cast out devils and take up serpents and to bring God's healing power to those who are sick and oppressed. I therefore make the following decrees, completely assured of both my identity and authority in Christ Jesus!

## 6. Loudly Declare These Supernatural Decrees So You Can Have Your Breakthrough:

- Heavenly Father I decree and declare that the power of the python spirit is completely broken over my life. I decree that I am no longer a victim of the python spirit, in Yeshua's name.

- I decree and declare that You are setting me free from every python spirit that causes physical and spiritual deafness in Yeshua's name.

- I decree and declare that the Holy Spirit is setting me free from the python spirit that has caused any kind of spiritual blindness in my life, in Yeshua's name, I pray.

- I decree and declare that the Holy Spirit is setting me free from the python spirit that would cause me not to walk in the truthfulness of God's Word, in Yeshua's name, I pray.

- I decree and declare that as I bring my sacrificial offering into the courts of Heaven, the power of the python spirit that satan placed over my finances is now destroyed, in Yeshua's name.

- I decree and declare that the python spirit covering my mind and stopping my spiritual and mental transformation according to Romans 12:1 is removed in Yeshua's mighty name!

- I decree and declare that God is setting me free from the python spirit, which has caused me to be spiritually crippled in Yeshua's name, I pray.

- I decree and declare that everything, which has been stolen from my life because of the python spirit, will now be restored back to me, in Yeshua's name, I pray.

## 7. End with Thanksgiving

Heavenly Father and Righteous Judge, I thank You that the foundation of Your throne is righteousness and justice. Thank You for giving me justice against the demonic entities behind the python spirit. Heavenly Father, I thank You that because of the finished work of Yeshua on the Cross, You have translated me from the kingdom of darkness to Your glorious Kingdom of Light! Heavenly Father, since You have adopted me into Your divine family, I thank You that You always hear me, when I pray. I thank You that every apostolic and prophetic decree that I have made has been heard. Thank You, Lord, that everything I have just decreed is on its way to full manifestation in Yeshua's mighty name. Heavenly Father, until the manifestation, I will maintain an aggressive attitude of thanksgiving for the complete manifestation of what I have decreed today! In Yeshua's name I pray.

PRAYER #8

# Decrees for Releasing the Glory

When Solomon had finished praying, fire came down from heaven and consumed the burnt offering and the sacrifices; and the glory of the Lord filled the temple. And the priests could not enter the house of the Lord, because the glory of the Lord had filled the Lord's house (**2 Chronicles 7:1-2 NKJV**).

## Prayer of Activation

### 1. Worship God

Heavenly Father, holy is Your name and greatly to be praised. You are the Father of Light and in You is no shadow of turning. I worship and adore You in Yeshua's name, for this purpose was I created, to give You pleasure through my love and adoration. May Your Kingdom manifest in my life as it is in Heaven. Plead my cause, O Lord, with those who strive with me; fight against any entity or person who is contending against me and what is written about me in Your book of destiny. Heavenly Father, it is written in Psalm 27:6 (NASB), *"And now my head will be lifted up above my enemies around me, and I will offer sacrifices in His tent with shouts of joy; I will sing, yes, I will sing praises to the Lord."* Heavenly Father, I thank You that I will never be swallowed by the demonic powers because You are the

Lifter of my head. Abba Father, I enjoin my worship to the heavenly chorus of worship of Your holy angels and the crowd of witnesses, in Yeshua's mighty name.

## 2. Enter the Courts of Heaven

Heavenly Father, Righteous Judge, I ask that the courts of Heaven be seated according to Daniel 7:9-10 (AMP) and that all books related to my life and destiny be opened. I ask this in Yeshua's mighty name. It is written: *"I kept looking until thrones were set up, and the Ancient of Days (God) took His seat; His garment was white as snow and the hair of His head like pure wool. His throne was flames of fire; its wheels were a burning fire. A river of fire was flowing and coming out from before Him; a thousand thousands were attending Him, and ten thousand times ten thousand were standing before Him; the court was seated, and the books were opened."* Heavenly Father, Righteous Judge, I am requesting the privilege of standing before the courtroom of the Ancient of Days according to what was revealed to the prophet Daniel, in Yeshua's name, I pray. Heavenly Father, I stand in Your royal courtroom because of the shed blood and finished work of Yeshua on the Cross. I have come to receive Your righteous judgment over my life against every evil tactic that satan has been using against me to stop me from releasing the glory. Heavenly Father, I call upon Your holy angels to be witnesses to my lawsuit and righteous prosecution of every evil tactic that satan has been using against me to stop me from releasing the glory. I decree and declare that every evil tactic that satan has been using against me to stop me from releasing the glory in my spirit, soul, and body will be removed so I can achieve my God-given destiny here on earth, in Yeshua's name I pray.

## 3. Repent

Heavenly Father, Righteous Judge, it is written, *"If we confess our sins, He is faithful and just to forgive us our sins and to cleanse us from all unrighteousness"* (1 John 1:9 NKJV). I therefore activate the law of repentance and present before this court my heartfelt repentance for my personal transgressions, and for the iniquities of my forefathers that opened the door for every veil of darkness to oppress my life and bloodline, in Yeshua's name I pray. Heavenly Father, I ask that the blood of Yeshua wash away every iniquity of my forefathers that the enemy is using as a legal right to build cases against me and to bind me to every evil tactic that satan has been using against me to stop me from releasing the glory. I also repent for all self-inflicted word curses and covenants with demons that have existed in my ancestral bloodline. I am asking that every ancestral agreement with demonic powers and evil altars will now be revoked. I petition the courts of Heaven to silence their right to claim me and my bloodline, in Yeshua's name. Thank You, Lord, for revoking these demonically engineered covenants and evil altars in Yeshua's mighty name! Heavenly Father and Righteous Judge, it is my heartfelt desire to divorce myself from every evil tactic that satan has been using against me to stop me from releasing the glory, that is operating in my life. I petition the Ancient of Days to grant me a verdict of judicial emancipation from the oppressive power of every evil tactic that satan has been using against me to stop me from releasing the glory. I receive Your favorable verdict by faith in Messiah's finished work and shed blood.

## 4. Petition the Courts of Heaven to Dismiss All of Satan's Charges

Heavenly Father and Righteous Judge, based upon Yeshua's finished work and my heartfelt repentance, I now move on the court of Heaven to dismiss all of satan's accusations and charges against me and my bloodline in Jesus's name. Righteous Judge, dismiss every one of satan's accusation connected to every evil tactic that satan has been using against me to stop me from releasing the glory. For it is written in Revelation 12:10 that the accuser of the brethren has been cast down. So, I petition You, Heavenly Father and

Righteous Judge, to cast down all of satan's accusations against me and dismiss all of satan's charges against me, in Yeshua's name, I pray.

## 5. Declare Your Authority in Christ

Heavenly Father and Righteous Judge, in Luke 10:19 (NKJV), Yeshua says, *"Behold, I give you the authority to trample on serpents and scorpions, and over all the power of the enemy, and nothing shall by any means hurt you."* Heavenly Father, as I prepare myself to pronounce powerful apostolic and prophetic decrees, I totally acknowledge my God-given authority in Christ to trample on serpents and scorpions that satan has weaponized against me and my destiny, in Yeshua's mighty name, I pray. The Bible also says in Proverbs 28:1 (NKJV), *"The wicked flee when no one pursues, but the righteous are bold as a lion."* Heavenly Father because of my God-given authority in Christ, I am as bold as lion. No messenger of satan, human or demonic, can intimidate me. I am like Mount Zion, which cannot be moved, in Yeshua's mighty name, I pray. I thank You, heavenly Father, that in Mark 16:17-18, Yeshua gave me the authority to cast out devils and take up serpents and to bring God's healing power to those who are sick and oppressed. I therefore make the following decrees, completely assured of both my identity and authority in Christ Jesus!

## 6. Loudly Declare These Supernatural Decrees So You Can Have Your Breakthrough:

- Heavenly Father, I decree and declare that the power of every evil tactic that satan has been using against me to stop me from releasing the glory is completely broken over my life. I decree that I am no longer a victim of these demonic evil tactics that satan has been using against me to stop me from releasing the glory, in Yeshua's name.

- I decree and declare that You are setting me free from every evil tactic that satan has been using against me to stop me from releasing the glory, that causes physical and spiritual deafness in Yeshua's name.

- I decree and declare that the Holy Spirit is setting me free from any veil of witchcraft or magic that has caused any kind of spiritual blindness in my life, in Yeshua's name, I pray.

- I decree and declare that the Holy Spirit is setting me free from every evil tactic that satan has been using against me to stop me from releasing the glory that has caused me not to walk in the truthfulness of God's Word, in Yeshua's name, I pray.

- I decree and declare that as I bring my sacrificial offering into the courts of Heaven, the power of every evil tactic that satan has been using against me to stop me from releasing the glory of God over my finances is now destroyed, in Yeshua's name.

- I decree and declare that every evil tactic that satan has been using against me to stop me from releasing the glory and stopping my spiritual and mental transformation according to Romans 12:1 is removed in Yeshua's mighty name!

- I decree and declare that God is setting me free from every evil tactic that satan has been using against me to stop me from releasing the glory, which has caused me to be spiritually crippled in Yeshua's name, I pray.

- I decree and declare that everything, which has been stolen from my life because of evil tactics that satan has been using against me to stop me from releasing the glory, will now be restored back to me, in Yeshua's name, I pray.

## 7. End with Thanksgiving

Heavenly Father and Righteous Judge, I thank You that the foundation of Your throne is righteousness and justice. Thank You for giving me justice against the demonic entities behind evil tactic that satan has been using against me to stop me from releasing the glory of God. Heavenly Father, I thank You that because of the finished work of Yeshua on the Cross, You have translated me from the kingdom of darkness to your glorious Kingdom of Light! Heavenly Father, since You have adopted me into Your divine family, I thank You that always hear me, when I pray. I thank You that every apostolic and prophetic decree that I have made has been heard. Thank You, Lord, that everything I have just decreed is on its way to full manifestation in Yeshua's mighty name. Heavenly Father, until the manifestation, I will maintain an aggressive attitude of thanksgiving for the complete manifestation of what I have decreed today! In Yeshua's name I pray.

# Decrees for Overthrowing Free Masonry

The ironsmith shapes iron and uses a chisel and works it over the coals. He forms the [idol's] core with hammers and works it with his strong arm. He also becomes hungry and his strength fails; he drinks no water and grows tired. The carpenter stretches out a measuring line, he marks out the shape [of the idol] with red chalk; he works it with planes and outlines it with the compass; and he makes it like the form of a man, like the beauty of man, that it may sit in a house (**Isaiah 44:12-13 AMP**).

## Prayer of Activation

### 1. Worship God

Heavenly Father, holy is Your name and greatly to be praised. You are the Father of Light and in You is no shadow of turning. I worship and adore You in Yeshua's name, for this purpose was I created, to give You pleasure through my love and adoration. May Your Kingdom manifest in my life as it is in Heaven. Plead my cause, O Lord, with those who strive with me; fight against any entity or person who is contending against me and what is written about me in Your book of destiny. Heavenly Father, it is written in Psalm 27:6 (NASB), *"And now my head will be lifted up above*

*my enemies around me, and I will offer sacrifices in His tent with shouts of joy; I will sing, yes, I will sing praises to the Lord."* Heavenly Father, I thank You that I will never be swallowed by the demonic powers because You are the Lifter of my head. Abba Father, I enjoin my worship to the heavenly chorus of worship of Your holy angels and the crowd of witnesses, in Yeshua's mighty name.

## 2. Enter the Courts of Heaven

Heavenly Father, Righteous Judge, I ask that the courts of Heaven be seated according to Daniel 7:9-10 (AMP) and that all books related to my life and destiny be opened. I ask this in Yeshua's mighty name. It is written: *"I kept looking until thrones were set up, and the Ancient of Days (God) took His seat; His garment was white as snow and the hair of His head like pure wool. His throne was flames of fire; its wheels were a burning fire. A river of fire was flowing and coming out from before Him; a thousand thousands were attending Him, and ten thousand times ten thousand were standing before Him; the court was seated, and the books were opened."* Heavenly Father, Righteous Judge, I am requesting the privilege of standing before the courtroom of the Ancient of Days according to what was revealed to the prophet Daniel, in Yeshua's name, I pray. Heavenly Father, I stand in Your royal courtroom because of the shed blood and finished work of Yeshua on the Cross. I have come to receive Your righteous judgment over my life against every form of free masonry that satan has been using against me. Heavenly Father, I call upon Your holy angels to be witnesses to my lawsuit and righteous prosecution of every form of free masonry that is working against me. I decree and declare that every form of free masonry covering my spirit, soul, and body will be removed so I can achieve my God-given destiny here on earth, in Yeshua's name I pray.

## 3. Repent

Heavenly Father, Righteous Judge, it is written, *"If we confess our sins, He is faithful and just to forgive us our sins and to cleanse us from all unrighteousness"* (1 John 1:9 NKJV). I therefore activate the law of repentance and present before this court my heartfelt repentance for my personal transgressions, and for the iniquities of my forefathers that opened the door for every form of free masonry to oppress my life and bloodline, in Yeshua's name I pray. Heavenly Father, I ask that the blood of Yeshua wash away every iniquity of my forefathers that the enemy is using as a legal right to build cases against me and to bind me to every form of free masonry. I also repent for all self-inflicted word curses and covenants with demons that have existed in my ancestral bloodline. I am asking that every ancestral agreement with demonic powers and evil altars will now be revoked. I petition the courts of Heaven to silence their right to claim me and my bloodline, in Yeshua's name. Thank You, Lord, for revoking these demonically engineered covenants and evil altars in Yeshua's mighty name! Heavenly Father and Righteous Judge, it is my heartfelt desire to divorce myself from every form of free masonry that is operating in my life. I petition the Ancient of Days to grant me a verdict of judicial emancipation from the oppressive power of every form of free masonry. I receive Your favorable verdict by faith in Messiah's finished work and shed blood.

## 4. Petition the Courts of Heaven to Dismiss All of Satan's Charges

Heavenly Father and Righteous Judge, based upon Yeshua's finished work and my heartfelt repentance, I now move on the Court of Heaven to dismiss all of satan's accusations and charges against me and my bloodline in Jesus's name. Righteous Judge, dismiss every one of satan's accusation connected to every form of free masonry that is oppressing my life. For it is written in Revelation 12:10 that the accuser of the brethren has been cast down. So, I petition You, heavenly Father and Righteous Judge, to cast down all of

satan's accusations against me and dismiss all of satan's charges against me, in Yeshua's name, I pray.

## 5. Declare Your Authority in Christ

Heavenly Father and Righteous Judge, in Luke 10:19 (NKJV), Yeshua says, *"Behold, I give you the authority to trample on serpents and scorpions, and over all the power of the enemy, and nothing shall by any means hurt you."* Heavenly Father. as I prepare myself to pronounce powerful apostolic and prophetic decrees, I totally acknowledge my God-given authority in Christ to trample on serpents and scorpions that satan has weaponized against me and my destiny, in Yeshua's mighty name, I pray. The Bible also says in Proverbs 28:1 (NKJV), *"The wicked flee when no one pursues, but the righteous are bold as a lion."* Heavenly Father, because of my God-given authority in Christ, I am as bold as lion. No messenger of satan, human or demonic, can intimidate me. I am like Mount Zion, which cannot be moved, in Yeshua's mighty name, I pray. I thank You, heavenly Father, that in Mark 16:17-18, Yeshua gave me the authority to cast out devils and take up serpents and to bring God's healing power to those who are sick and oppressed. I therefore make the following decrees, completely assured of both my identity and authority in Christ Jesus!

## 6. Loudly Declare These Supernatural Decrees So You Can Have Your Breakthrough:

- Heavenly Father, I decree and declare that the power of every form of free masonry is completely broken over my life. I decree that I am no longer a victim of any form of free masonry, in Yeshua's name.

- I decree and declare that You are setting me free from every form of free masonry that causes physical and spiritual deafness in Yeshua's name.

- I decree and declare that the Holy Spirit is setting me free from any form of free masonry that has caused any kind of spiritual blindness in my life, in Yeshua's name, I pray.

- I decree and declare that the Holy Spirit is setting me free from every veil of deception caused by free masonry in my bloodline that would cause me not to walk in the truthfulness of God's Word, in Yeshua's name, I pray.

- I decree and declare that as I bring my sacrificial offering into the courts of Heaven, the power of every form of free masonry that satan placed over my finances is now destroyed, in Yeshua's name.

- I decree and declare that every form of free masonry covering my mind and stopping my spiritual and mental transformation according to Romans 12:1 is removed in Yeshua's mighty name!

- I decree and declare that God is setting me free from every form of free masonry, which has caused me to be spiritually crippled in Yeshua's name, I pray.

- I decree and declare that everything, which has been stolen from my life because of any form of free masonry in my bloodline, will now be restored back to me, in Yeshua's name, I pray.

## 7. End with Thanksgiving

Heavenly Father and Righteous Judge, I thank You that the foundation of Your throne is righteousness and justice. Thank You for giving me justice against the demonic entities behind every form of free masonry that is afflicting me. Heavenly Father, I thank You that because of the finished work of Yeshua on the Cross, You have translated me from the kingdom of darkness to Your glorious Kingdom of Light! Heavenly Father, since You have adopted me into your divine family, I thank You that You always hear me, when I pray. I thank You that every apostolic and prophetic decree that I have made has been heard. Thank You, Lord, that everything I have just decreed is on its way to full manifestation in Yeshua's mighty name. Heavenly Father, until the manifestation, I will maintain an aggressive attitude of thanksgiving for the complete manifestation of what I have decreed today! In Yeshua's name I pray.

# Decrees for Overthrowing Spirit Husbands

When the human race began to increase, with more and more daughters being born, the sons of God noticed that the daughters of men were beautiful. They looked them over and picked out wives for themselves. Then God said, "I'm not going to breathe life into men and women endlessly. Eventually they're going to die; from now on they can expect a life span of 120 years." This was back in the days (and also later) when there were giants in the land. The giants came from the union of the sons of God and the daughters of men. These were the mighty men of ancient lore, the famous ones (Genesis 6:1-4 The Message).

## Prayer of Activation

### 1. Worship God

Heavenly Father, holy is Your name and greatly to be praised. You are the Father of Light and in You is no shadow of turning. I worship and adore You in Yeshua's name, for this purpose was I created, to give You pleasure through my love and adoration. May Your Kingdom manifest in my life as it is in Heaven. Plead my cause, O Lord, with those who strive with me; fight against any entity or person who is contending against me and what is written about me in Your book of destiny. Heavenly Father, it is written in Psalm 27:6 (NASB), *"And now my head will be lifted up above my enemies around me, and I will offer sacrifices in His tent with shouts of joy; I will sing, yes, I will sing praises to the Lord."* Heavenly Father, I thank You that I will never be swallowed by the demonic powers because You are the Lifter of my head. Abba Father, I enjoin my worship to the heavenly chorus of worship of Your holy angels and the crowd of witnesses, in Yeshua's mighty name.

## 2. Enter the Courts of Heaven

Heavenly Father, Righteous Judge, I ask that the courts of Heaven be seated according to Daniel 7:9-10 (AMP) and that all books related to my life and destiny be opened. I ask this in Yeshua's mighty name. It is written: *"I kept looking until thrones were set up, and the Ancient of Days (God) took His seat; His garment was white as snow and the hair of His head like pure wool. His throne was flames of fire; its wheels were a burning fire. A river of fire was flowing and coming out from before Him; a thousand thousands were attending Him, and ten thousand times ten thousand were standing before Him; the court was seated, and the books were opened."* Heavenly Father, Righteous Judge, I am requesting the privilege of standing before the courtroom of the Ancient of Days according to what was revealed to the prophet Daniel, in Yeshua's name, I pray. Heavenly Father, I stand in Your royal courtroom because of the shed blood and finished work of Yeshua on the Cross. I have come to receive Your righteous judgment over my life against every spirit husband that satan has been using against me. Heavenly Father, I call upon Your holy angels to be witnesses to my lawsuit and righteous prosecution of every spirit husband that is working against me. I decree and declare that every spirit husband covering my spirit, soul, and body will be removed so I can achieve my God-given destiny here on earth, in Yeshua's name I pray.

## 3. Repent

Heavenly Father, Righteous Judge, it is written, *"If we confess our sins, He is faithful and just to forgive us our sins and to cleanse us from all unrighteousness"* (1 John 1:9 NKJV). I therefore activate the law of repentance and present before this court my heartfelt repentance for my personal transgressions, and for the iniquities of my forefathers that opened the door for every veil of darkness to oppress my life and bloodline, in Yeshua's name I pray. Heavenly Father, I ask that the blood of Yeshua wash away every iniquity of my forefathers that the enemy is using as a legal right to build cases against me and to bind me to any spirit husband. I also repent for all self-inflicted word curses and covenants with demons that have existed in my ancestral bloodline. I am asking that every ancestral agreement with demonic powers and evil altars will now be revoked. I petition the courts of Heaven to silence their right to claim me and my bloodline, in Yeshua's name. Thank You, Lord, for revoking these demonically engineered covenants and evil altars in Yeshua's mighty name! Heavenly Father and Righteous Judge, it is my heartfelt desire to divorce myself from any spirit husband that is operating in my life. I petition the Ancient of Days to grant me a verdict of judicial emancipation from the oppressive power of any spirit husband. I receive Your favorable verdict by faith in Messiah's finished work and shed blood.

## 4. Petition the Courts of Heaven to Dismiss All of Satan's Charges

Heavenly Father and Righteous Judge, based upon Yeshua's finished work and my heartfelt repentance, I now move on the Court of Heaven to dismiss all of satan's accusations and charges against me and my bloodline in Jesus's name. Righteous Judge, dismiss every one of satan's accusation connected to any spirit husband that is oppressing my life. For it is written in Revelation

12:10 that the accuser of the brethren has been cast down. So, I petition You, heavenly Father and Righteous Judge, to cast down all of satan's accusations against me and dismiss all of satan's charges against me, in Yeshua's name, I pray.

## 5. Declare Your Authority in Christ

Heavenly Father and Righteous Judge, in Luke 10:19 (NKJV), Yeshua says, *"Behold, I give you the authority to trample on serpents and scorpions, and over all the power of the enemy, and nothing shall by any means hurt you."* Heavenly Father, as I prepare myself to pronounce powerful apostolic and prophetic decrees, I totally acknowledge my God-given authority in Christ to trample on serpents and scorpions that satan has weaponized against me and my destiny, in Yeshua's mighty name, I pray. The Bible also says in Proverbs 28:1 (NKJV), *"The wicked flee when no one pursues, but the righteous are bold as a lion."* Heavenly Father because of my God-given authority in Christ, I am as bold as lion. No messenger of satan, human or demonic, can intimidate me. I am like Mount Zion, which cannot be moved, in Yeshua's mighty name, I pray. I thank You, heavenly Father, that in Mark 16:17-18, Yeshua gave me the authority to cast out devils and take up serpents and to bring God's healing power to those who are sick and oppressed. I therefore make the following decrees, completely assured of both my identity and authority in Christ Jesus!

## 6. Loudly Declare These Supernatural Decrees So You Can Have Your Breakthrough:

- Heavenly Father, I decree and declare that the power of any spirit husband to sexually molest me at night, is completely broken over my life. I decree that I am no longer a victim of any spirit husband, in Yeshua's name.

- I decree and declare that You are setting me free from any spirit husband that causes physical and spiritual deafness in Yeshua's name.

- I decree and declare that the Holy Spirit is setting me free from any spirit husband that has caused any kind of spiritual blindness in my life, in Yeshua's name, I pray.

- I decree and declare that the Holy Spirit is setting me free from any spirit husband that would cause me not to walk in the truthfulness of God's Word, in Yeshua's name, I pray.

- I decree and declare that as I bring my sacrificial offering into the courts of Heaven, the power of any spirit husband that satan placed over my finances is now destroyed, in Yeshua's name.

- I decree and declare that any spirit husband stopping my spiritual and mental transformation according to Romans 12:1 is removed in Yeshua's mighty name!

- I decree and declare that God is setting me free from any spirit husband that has caused me to be spiritually crippled in Yeshua's name, I pray.

- I decree and declare that everything, which has been stolen from my life because of the evil spirit husband, will now be restored back to me, in Yeshua's name, I pray.

## 7. End with Thanksgiving

Heavenly Father and Righteous Judge, I thank You that the foundation of Your throne is righteousness and justice. Thank You for giving me justice against the demonic entities behind the evil spirit husband. Heavenly Father,

I thank You that because of the finished work of Yeshua on the Cross, You have translated me from the kingdom of darkness to Your glorious Kingdom of Light! Heavenly Father, since You have adopted me into Your divine family, I thank You that You always hear me, when I pray. I thank You that every apostolic and prophetic decree that I have made has been heard. Thank You, Lord, that everything I have just decreed is on its way to full manifestation in Yeshua's mighty name. Heavenly Father, until the manifestation, I will maintain an aggressive attitude of thanksgiving for the complete manifestation of what I have decreed today! In Yeshua's name I pray.

# Decrees for Overthrowing Spirit Wives

When the human race began to increase, with more and more daughters being born, the sons of God noticed that the daughters of men were beautiful. They looked them over and picked out wives for themselves. Then God said, "I'm not going to breathe life into men and women endlessly. Eventually they're going to die; from now on they can expect a life span of 120 years." This was back in the days (and also later) when there were giants in the land. The giants came from the union of the sons of God and the daughters of men. These were the mighty men of ancient lore, the famous ones (Genesis 6:1-4 The Message).

## Prayer of Activation

### 1. Worship God

Heavenly Father, holy is Your name and greatly to be praised. You are the Father of Light and in You is no shadow of turning. I worship and adore You in Yeshua's name, for this purpose was I created, to give You pleasure through my love and adoration. May Your Kingdom manifest in my life as it is in Heaven. Plead my cause, O Lord, with those who strive with me; fight against any entity or person who is contending against me and what is written about me in Your book of destiny. Heavenly Father, it is written in Psalm 27:6 (NASB), *"And now my head will be lifted up above my enemies around me, and I will offer sacrifices in His tent with shouts of joy; I will sing, yes, I will sing praises to the Lord."* Heavenly Father, I thank You that I will never be swallowed by the demonic powers because You are the Lifter of my head. Abba Father, I enjoin my worship to the heavenly chorus of worship of Your holy angels and the crowd of witnesses, in Yeshua's mighty name.

## 2. Enter the Courts of Heaven

Heavenly Father, Righteous Judge, I ask that the courts of Heaven be seated according to Daniel 7:9-10 (AMP) and that all books related to my life and destiny be opened. I ask this in Yeshua's mighty name. It is written: *"I kept looking until thrones were set up, and the Ancient of Days (God) took His seat; His garment was white as snow and the hair of His head like pure wool. His throne was flames of fire; its wheels were a burning fire. A river of fire was flowing and coming out from before Him; a thousand thousands were attending Him, and ten thousand times ten thousand were standing before Him; the court was seated, and the books were opened."* Heavenly Father, Righteous Judge, I am requesting the privilege of standing before the courtroom of the Ancient of Days according to what was revealed to the prophet Daniel, in Yeshua's name, I pray. Heavenly Father, I stand in Your royal courtroom because of the shed blood and finished work of Yeshua on the Cross. I have come to receive Your righteous judgment over my life against every evil spirit wife satan has been using against me. Heavenly Father, I call upon Your holy angels to be witnesses to my lawsuit and righteous prosecution of every evil spirit wife that is working against me. I decree and declare that every evil spirit wife covering my spirit, soul, and body will be removed so I can achieve my God-given destiny here on earth, in Yeshua's name I pray.

## 3. Repent

Heavenly Father, Righteous Judge, it is written, *"If we confess our sins, He is faithful and just to forgive us our sins and to cleanse us from all unrighteousness"*(1 John 1:9 NKJV). I therefore activate the law of repentance and present before this court my heartfelt repentance for my personal transgressions, and for the iniquities of my forefathers that opened the door for every evil spirit wife to oppress my life and bloodline, in Yeshua's name I pray. Heavenly Father, I ask that the blood of Yeshua wash away every iniquity of my forefathers that the enemy is using as a legal right to build cases against me and to bind me to every evil spirit wife. I also repent for all self-inflicted word curses and covenants with demons that have existed in my ancestral bloodline. I am asking that every ancestral agreement with demonic powers and evil altars will now be revoked. I petition the courts of Heaven to silence their right to claim me and my bloodline, in Yeshua's name. Thank You, Lord, for revoking these demonically engineered covenants and evil altars in Yeshua's mighty name! Heavenly Father and Righteous Judge, it is my heartfelt desire to divorce myself from every evil spirit wife that is operating in my life. I petition the Ancient of Days to grant me a verdict of judicial emancipation from the oppressive power of every evil spirit wife. I receive Your favorable verdict by faith in Messiah's finished work and shed blood.

## 4. Petition the Courts of Heaven to Dismiss All of Satan's Charges

Heavenly Father and Righteous Judge, based upon Yeshua's finished work and my heartfelt repentance, I now move on the court of Heaven to dismiss all of satan's accusations and charges against me and my bloodline in Jesus's name. Righteous Judge, dismiss every one of satan's accusation connected to the evil spirit wife that is oppressing my life. For it is written in Revelation 12:10 that the accuser of the brethren has been cast down. So, I petition You, heavenly Father and Righteous Judge, to cast down all of satan's accusations

Dangerous Decrees That Destroy Strongholds

against me and dismiss all of satan's charges against me, in Yeshua's name, I pray.

## 5. Declare Your Authority in Christ

Heavenly Father and Righteous Judge, in Luke 10:19 (NKJV), Yeshua says, *"Behold, I give you the authority to trample on serpents and scorpions, and over all the power of the enemy, and nothing shall by any means hurt you."* Heavenly Father, as I prepare myself to pronounce powerful apostolic and prophetic decrees, I totally acknowledge my God-given authority in Christ to trample on serpents and scorpions that satan has weaponized against me and my destiny, in Yeshua's mighty name, I pray. The Bible also says in Proverbs 28:1 (NKJV), *"The wicked flee when no one pursues, but the righteous are bold as a lion."* Heavenly Father because of my God-given authority in Christ, I am as bold as lion. No messenger of satan, human or demonic, can intimidate me. I am like Mount Zion, which cannot be moved, in Yeshua's mighty name, I pray. I thank You, heavenly Father that in Mark 16:17-18, Yeshua gave me the authority to cast out devils and take up serpents and to bring God's healing power to those who are sick and oppressed. I therefore make the following decrees, completely assured of both my identity and authority in Christ Jesus!

## 6. Loudly Declare These Supernatural Decrees So You Can Have Your Breakthrough:

- Heavenly Father I decree and declare that the power of any evil spirit wife to sexually molest me at night is completely broken over my life. I decree that I am no longer a victim of any evil spirit wife, in Yeshua's name.

- I decree and declare that You are setting me free from any evil spirit wife that causes physical and spiritual deafness in Yeshua's name.

146

- I decree and declare that the Holy Spirit is setting me free from any evil spirit wife that has caused any kind of spiritual blindness in my life, in Yeshua's name, I pray.

- I decree and declare that the Holy Spirit is setting me free from any evil spirit wife that would cause me not to walk in the truthfulness of God's word, in Yeshua's name, I pray.

- I decree and declare that as I bring my sacrificial offering into the Courts of Heaven, the power of any evil spirit wife that satan placed over my finances is now destroyed, in Yeshua's name.

- I decree and declare that any evil spirit wife covering stopping my spiritual and mental transformation according to Romans 12:1 is removed in Yeshua's mighty name!

- I decree and declare that God is setting me free from any evil spirit wife that has caused me to be spiritually crippled in Yeshua's name, I pray.

- I decree and declare that everything, which has been stolen from my life because of any evil spirit wife, will now be restored back to me, in Yeshua's name, I pray.

## 7. End with Thanksgiving

Heavenly Father and Righteous Judge, I thank You that the foundation of Your throne is righteousness and justice. Thank You for giving me justice against the demonic entities behind any evil spirit wife. Heavenly Father, I thank You that because of the finished work of Yeshua on the Cross, You have translated me from the kingdom of darkness to Your glorious Kingdom of Light! Heavenly Father, since You have adopted me into Your divine family,

I thank You that You always hear me, when I pray. I thank You that every apostolic and prophetic decree that I have made has been heard. Thank You, Lord, that everything I have just decreed is on its way to full manifestation in Yeshua's mighty name. Heavenly Father, until the manifestation, I will maintain an aggressive attitude of thanksgiving for the complete manifestation of what I have decreed today! In Yeshua's name I pray.

PRAYER #12

# Decrees for Releasing Supernatural Favor

And I will grant this people favor and respect in the sight of the Egyptians; therefore, it shall be that when you go, you will not go empty-handed (**Exodus 3:21 AMP**).

## Prayer of Activation

### 1. Worship God

Heavenly Father, holy is Your name and greatly to be praised. You are the Father of Light and in You is no shadow of turning. I worship and adore You in Yeshua's name, for this purpose was I created, to give You pleasure through my love and adoration. May Your Kingdom manifest in my life as it is in Heaven. Plead my cause, O Lord, with those who strive with me; fight against any entity or person who is contending against me and what is written about me in Your book of destiny. Heavenly Father, it is written in Psalm 27:6 (NASB), *"And now my head will be lifted up above my enemies around me, and I will offer sacrifices in His tent with shouts of joy; I will sing, yes, I will sing praises to the Lord."* Heavenly Father, I thank You that I will never be swallowed by the demonic powers because You are the

Lifter of my head. Abba Father, I enjoin my worship to the heavenly chorus of worship of Your holy angels and the crowd of witnesses, in Yeshua's mighty name.

## 2. Enter the Courts of Heaven

Heavenly Father, Righteous Judge, I ask that the courts of Heaven be seated according to Daniel 7:9-10 (AMP) and that all books related to my life and destiny be opened. I ask this in Yeshua's mighty name. It is written: *"I kept looking until thrones were set up, and the Ancient of Days (God) took His seat; His garment was white as snow and the hair of His head like pure wool. His throne was flames of fire; its wheels were a burning fire. A river of fire was flowing and coming out from before Him; a thousand thousands were attending Him, and ten thousand times ten thousand were standing before Him; the court was seated, and the books were opened."* Heavenly Father, Righteous Judge, I am requesting the privilege of standing before the courtroom of the Ancient of Days according to what was revealed to the prophet Daniel, in Yeshua's name, I pray. Heavenly Father, I stand in Your royal courtroom because of the shed blood and finished work of Yeshua on the Cross. I have come to receive Your righteous judgment over my life against every evil scheme that satan has been using against me to stop me from walking in the favor of God. Heavenly Father, I call upon Your holy angels to be witnesses to my lawsuit and righteous prosecution of every evil scheme that satan has been using against me to stop from walking in the favor of God. I decree and declare that evil scheme that satan has been using against me to stop me from walking in the favor of God in my spirit, soul, and body will be removed so I can achieve my God-given destiny here on earth, in Yeshua's name I pray.

## 3. Repent

Heavenly Father, Righteous Judge, it is written, *"If we confess our sins, He is faithful and just to forgive us our sins and to cleanse us from all unrighteousness"*

(1 John 1:9 NKJV). I therefore activate the law of repentance and present before this court my heartfelt repentance for my personal transgressions, and for the iniquities of my forefathers that opened the door for every evil scheme that satan has been using against me to stop me from walking in the favor of God, in Yeshua's name I pray. Heavenly Father, I ask that the blood of Yeshua wash away every iniquity of my forefathers that the enemy is using as a legal right to build cases against me and to bind me to every evil scheme that satan has been using against me to stop me from walking in the favor of God. I also repent for all self-inflicted word curses and covenants with demons that have existed in my ancestral bloodline. I am asking that every ancestral agreement with demonic powers and evil altars will now be revoked. I petition the courts of Heaven to silence their right to claim me and my bloodline, in Yeshua's name. Thank You, Lord, for revoking these demonically engineered covenants and evil altars in Yeshua's mighty name! Heavenly Father and Righteous Judge, it is my heartfelt desire to divorce myself from every evil scheme that satan has been using against me to stop me from walking in the favor of God. I petition the Ancient of Days to grant me a verdict of judicial emancipation from the oppressive power of every evil scheme that satan has been using against me to stop me from walking in the favor of God. I receive Your favorable verdict by faith in Messiah's finished work and shed blood.

## 4. Petition the Courts of Heaven to Dismiss All of Satan's Charges

Heavenly Father and Righteous Judge, based upon Yeshua's finished work and my heartfelt repentance, I now move on the court of Heaven to dismiss all of satan's accusations and charges against me and my bloodline in Jesus's name. Righteous Judge, dismiss every one of satan's accusation connected to every evil scheme that satan has been using against me to stop me from walking in the favor of God. For it is written in Revelation 12:10 that the accuser of the brethren has been cast down. So, I petition You, heavenly Father and

Righteous Judge, to cast down all of satan's accusations against me and dismiss all of satan's charges against me, in Yeshua's name, I pray.

## 5. Declare Your Authority in Christ

Heavenly Father and Righteous Judge, in Luke 10:19 (NKJV), Yeshua says, *"Behold, I give you the authority to trample on serpents and scorpions, and over all the power of the enemy, and nothing shall by any means hurt you."* Heavenly Father, as I prepare myself to pronounce powerful apostolic and prophetic decrees, I totally acknowledge my God-given authority in Christ to trample on serpents and scorpions that satan has weaponized against me and my destiny, in Yeshua's mighty name, I pray. The Bible also says in Proverbs 28:1 (NKJV), *"The wicked flee when no one pursues, but the righteous are bold as a lion."* Heavenly Father because of my God-given authority in Christ, I am as bold as lion. No messenger of satan, human or demonic, can intimidate me. I am like Mount Zion, which cannot be moved, in Yeshua's mighty name, I pray. I thank You, heavenly Father, that in Mark 16:17-18, Yeshua gave me the authority to cast out devils and take up serpents and to bring God's healing power to those who are sick and oppressed. I therefore make the following decrees, completely assured of both my identity and authority in Christ Jesus!

## 6. Loudly Declare These Supernatural Decrees So You Can Have Your Breakthrough:

- Heavenly Father, I decree and declare that the power of every evil scheme that satan has been using against me to stop me from walking in the favor of God is completely broken over my life. I decree that I am no longer a victim of these demonic schemes that satan has been using against me to stop me from walking in the favor of God, in Yeshua's name.

- I decree and declare that You are setting me free from evil scheme that satan has been using against me to stop me from walking in the favor of God that causes physical and spiritual poverty in Yeshua's name.

- I decree and declare that the Holy Spirit is setting me free from any evil scheme that satan has been using against me to stop me from walking in the favor of God that has caused any kind of spiritual blindness in my life, in Yeshua's name, I pray.

- I decree and declare that the Holy Spirit is setting me free from every evil scheme that satan has been using against me to stop me from walking in the favor of God that would cause me not to walk in the truthfulness of God's word, in Yeshua's name, I pray.

- I decree and declare that as I bring my sacrificial offering into the courts of Heaven, the power of every evil scheme that satan has been using against me to stop me from walking in the favor of God that satan placed over my finances is now destroyed, in Yeshua's name.

- I decree and declare that every evil scheme that satan has been using against me to stop me from walking in the favor of God that are stopping my spiritual and mental transformation according to Romans 12:1 is removed in Yeshua's mighty name!

- I decree and declare that God is setting me free from every evil scheme that satan has been using against me to stop me from walking in the favor of God, which has caused me to be spiritually and financially crippled in Yeshua's name, I pray.

- I decree and declare that everything, which has been stolen from my life because of every evil scheme that satan has been using against me to stop me from walking in the favor of God, will now be restored back to me, in Yeshua's name, I pray.

## 7. End with Thanksgiving

Heavenly Father and Righteous Judge, I thank You that the foundation of Your throne is righteousness and justice. Thank You for giving me justice against the demonic entities behind these evil schemes that satan has been using against me to stop me from walking in the favor of God. Heavenly Father, I thank You that because of the finished work of Yeshua on the Cross, You have translated me from the kingdom of darkness to Your glorious Kingdom of Light! Heavenly Father, since You have adopted me into Your divine family, I thank You that You always hear me, when I pray. I thank You that every apostolic and prophetic decree that I have made has been heard. Thank You, Lord, that everything I have just decreed is on its way to full manifestation in Yeshua's mighty name. Heavenly Father, until the manifestation, I will maintain an aggressive attitude of thanksgiving for the complete manifestation of what I have decreed today! In Yeshua's name I pray.

# Decrees for Uprooting Evil Trees

Even so, every healthy tree bears good fruit, but the unhealthy tree bears bad fruit. A good tree cannot bear bad fruit, nor can a bad tree bear good fruit. Every tree that does not bear good fruit is cut down and thrown into the fire (**Matthew 7:17-19 AMP**).

## Prayer of Activation

### 1. Worship God

Heavenly Father, holy is Your name and greatly to be praised. You are the Father of Light and in You is no shadow of turning. I worship and adore You in Yeshua's name, for this purpose was I created, to give You pleasure through my love and adoration. May Your Kingdom manifest in my life as it is in Heaven. Plead my cause, O Lord, with those who strive with me; fight against any entity or person who is contending against me and what is written about me in Your book of destiny. Heavenly Father, it is written in Psalm 27:6 (NASB), *"And now my head will be lifted up above my enemies around me, and I will offer sacrifices in His tent with shouts of joy; I will sing, yes, I will sing praises to the Lord."* Heavenly Father, I thank You that I will never be swallowed by the demonic powers because You are the lifter of my head. Abba Father, I enjoin my worship to the heavenly chorus of

worship of Your holy angels and the crowd of witnesses, in Yeshua's mighty name.

## 2. Enter the Courts of Heaven

Heavenly Father, Righteous Judge, I ask that the courts of Heaven be seated according to Daniel 7:9-10 (AMP) and that all books related to my life and destiny be opened. I ask this in Yeshua's mighty name. It is written: *"I kept looking until thrones were set up, and the Ancient of Days (God) took His seat; His garment was white as snow and the hair of His head like pure wool. His throne was flames of fire; its wheels were a burning fire. A river of fire was flowing and coming out from before Him; a thousand thousands were attending Him, and ten thousand times ten thousand were standing before Him; the court was seated, and the books were opened."* Heavenly Father, Righteous Judge, I am requesting the privilege of standing before the courtroom of the Ancient of Days according to what was revealed to the prophet Daniel, in Yeshua's name, I pray. Heavenly Father, I stand in Your royal courtroom because of the shed blood and finished work of Yeshua on the Cross. I have come to receive Your righteous judgment over my life against every evil tree that satan has been using against me. Heavenly Father, I call upon Your holy angels to be witnesses to my lawsuit and righteous prosecution of every evil tree that is working against me. I decree and declare that every evil tree covering my spirit, soul, and body will be removed so I can achieve my God-given destiny here on earth, in Yeshua's name I pray.

## 3. Repent

Heavenly Father, Righteous Judge, it is written, *"If we confess our sins, He is faithful and just to forgive us our sins and to cleanse us from all unrighteousness"* (1 John 1:9 NKJV). I therefore activate the law of repentance and present before this court my heartfelt repentance for my personal transgressions, and for the iniquities of my forefathers that opened the door for every evil tree to oppress my life and bloodline, in Yeshua's name I pray. Heavenly Father, I ask that the blood of Yeshua wash away every iniquity of my forefathers that the enemy is using as a legal right to build cases against me and to bind me to every evil tree of darkness. I also repent for all self-inflicted word curses and covenants with demons that have existed in my ancestral bloodline. I am asking that every ancestral agreement with demonic powers and evil altars will now be revoked. I petition the courts of Heaven to silence their right to claim me and my bloodline, in Yeshua's name. Thank You, Lord, for revoking these demonically engineered covenants and evil altars in Yeshua's mighty name! Heavenly Father and Righteous Judge, it is my heartfelt desire to divorce myself from every evil tree of darkness that is operating in my life. I petition the Ancient of Days to grant me a verdict of judicial emancipation from the oppressive power of every evil tree of darkness. I receive Your favorable verdict by faith in Messiah's finished work and shed blood.

## 4. Petition the Courts of Heaven to Dismiss All of Satan's Charges

Heavenly Father and Righteous Judge, based upon Yeshua's finished work and my heartfelt repentance, I now move on the court of Heaven to dismiss all of satan's accusations and charges against me and my bloodline in Jesus's name. Righteous Judge, dismiss every one of satan's accusation connected to every evil tree that is oppressing my life. For it is written in Revelation 12:10 that the accuser of the brethren has been cast down. So, I petition You, heavenly Father and Righteous Judge, to cast down all of satan's accusations against me and dismiss all of satan's charges against me, in Yeshua's name, I pray.

## 5. Declare Your Authority in Christ

Heavenly Father and Righteous Judge, in Luke 10:19 (NKJV), Yeshua says, *"Behold, I give you the authority to trample on serpents and scorpions, and over all the power of the enemy, and nothing shall by any means hurt you."* Heavenly

Father, as I prepare myself to pronounce powerful apostolic and prophetic decrees, I totally acknowledge my God-given authority in Christ to trample on serpents and scorpions that satan has weaponized against me and my destiny, in Yeshua's mighty name, I pray. The Bible also says in Proverbs 28:1 (NKJV), "*The wicked flee when no one pursues, but the righteous are bold as a lion.*" Heavenly Father, because of my God-given authority in Christ, I am as bold as lion. No messenger of satan, human or demonic, can intimidate me. I am like Mount Zion, which cannot be moved, in Yeshua's mighty name, I pray. I thank You, heavenly Father that in Mark 16:17-18, Yeshua gave me the authority to cast out devils and take up serpents and to bring God's healing power to those who are sick and oppressed. I therefore make the following decrees, completely assured of both my identity and authority in Christ Jesus!

## 6. Loudly Declare These Supernatural Decrees So You Can Have Your Breakthrough:

- Heavenly Father, I decree and declare that the power of every evil tree of darkness is completely broken over my life. I decree that I am no longer a victim of these demonic evil trees of darkness, in Yeshua's name.

- I decree and declare that You are setting me free from every evil tree that causes physical and spiritual deafness in Yeshua's name.

- I decree and declare that the Holy Spirit is setting me free from any evil tree of witchcraft or magic that has caused any kind of spiritual blindness in my life, in Yeshua's name, I pray.

- I decree and declare that the Holy Spirit is setting me free from every evil tree of deception that would cause me not to walk in the truthfulness of God's Word, in Yeshua's name, I pray.

- I decree and declare that as I bring my sacrificial offering into the courts of Heaven, the power of every evil tree that satan placed over my finances is now destroyed, in Yeshua's name.

- I decree and declare that every evil tree of darkness covering my mind and stopping my spiritual and mental transformation according to Romans 12:1 is removed in Yeshua's mighty name!

- I decree and declare that God is setting me free from every evil tree, which has caused me to be spiritually crippled in Yeshua's name, I pray.

- I decree and declare that everything, which has been stolen from my life because of every evil tree of darkness, will now be restored back to me, in Yeshua's name, I pray.

## 7. End with Thanksgiving

Heavenly Father and Righteous Judge, I thank You that the foundation of Your throne is righteousness and justice. Thank You for giving me justice against the demonic entities behind these evil trees of darkness. Heavenly Father, I thank You that because of the finished work of Yeshua on the Cross, You have translated me from the kingdom of darkness to Your glorious Kingdom of Light! Heavenly Father, since You have adopted me into Your divine family, I thank You that You always hear me, when I pray. I thank You that every apostolic and prophetic decree that I have made has been heard. Thank You, Lord, that everything I have just decreed is on its way to full manifestation in Yeshua's mighty name. Heavenly Father, until the manifestation, I will maintain an aggressive attitude of thanksgiving for the complete manifestation of what I have decreed today! In Yeshua's name I pray.

# Decrees for Arresting Premature Death

I will not die, but live, and declare the works and recount the illustrious acts of the Lord (**Psalm 118:17 AMP**).

## Prayer of Activation

### 1. Worship God

Heavenly Father, holy is Your name and greatly to be praised. You are the Father of Light and in You is no shadow of turning. I worship and adore You in Yeshua's name, for this purpose was I created, to give You pleasure through my love and adoration. May Your Kingdom manifest in my life as it is in Heaven. Plead my cause, O Lord, with those who strive with me; fight against any entity or person who is contending against me and what is written about me in Your book of destiny. Heavenly Father, it is written in Psalm 27:6 (NASB), *"And now my head will be lifted up above my enemies around me, and I will offer sacrifices in His tent with shouts of joy; I will sing, yes, I will sing praises to the Lord."* Heavenly Father, I thank You that I will never be swallowed by the demonic powers because You are the Lifter of my head. Abba Father, I enjoin my worship to the heavenly chorus of worship of Your holy angels and the crowd of witnesses, in Yeshua's mighty name.

## 2. Enter the Courts of Heaven

Heavenly Father, Righteous Judge, I ask that the courts of Heaven be seated according to Daniel 7:9-10 (AMP) and that all books related to my life and destiny be opened. I ask this in Yeshua's mighty name. It is written: *"I kept looking until thrones were set up, and the Ancient of Days (God) took His seat; His garment was white as snow and the hair of His head like pure wool. His throne was flames of fire; its wheels were a burning fire. A river of fire was flowing and coming out from before Him; a thousand thousands were attending Him, and ten thousand times ten thousand were standing before Him; the court was seated, and the books were opened."* Heavenly Father, Righteous Judge, I am requesting the privilege of standing before the courtroom of the Ancient of Days according to what was revealed to the prophet Daniel, in Yeshua's name, I pray. Heavenly Father, I stand in Your royal courtroom because of the shed blood and finished work of Yeshua on the Cross. I have come to receive Your righteous judgment over my life against every evil scheme of satan to bring about my premature death. Heavenly Father, I call upon Your holy angels to be witnesses to my lawsuit and righteous prosecution of every evil veil that is working against me. I decree and declare that every evil scheme of satan to bring about my premature death over my spirit, soul, and body will be removed so I can achieve my God-given destiny here on earth, in Yeshua's name I pray.

## 3. Repent

Heavenly Father, Righteous Judge, it is written, *"If we confess our sins, He is faithful and just to forgive us our sins and to cleanse us from all unrighteousness"* (1 John 1:9 NKJV). I therefore activate the law of repentance and present before this court my heartfelt repentance for my personal transgressions, and for the iniquities of my forefathers that opened the door for every veil of darkness to oppress my life and bloodline, in Yeshua's name I pray. Heavenly Father, I ask that the blood of Yeshua wash away every iniquity of my forefathers that the enemy is using as a legal right to build cases against me and to bind me to every evil scheme of satan to bring about my premature death. I also repent for all self-inflicted word curses and covenants with demons that have existed in my ancestral bloodline. I am asking that every ancestral agreement with demonic powers and evil altars will now be revoked. I petition the courts of Heaven to silence their right to claim me and my bloodline, in Yeshua's name. Thank You, Lord, for revoking these demonically engineered covenants and evil altars in Yeshua's mighty name! Heavenly Father and Righteous Judge, it is my heartfelt desire to divorce myself from every evil scheme of satan to bring about my premature death that is operating in my life. I petition the Ancient of Days to grant me a verdict of judicial emancipation from the oppressive power of every evil scheme of satan to bring about my premature death. I receive Your favorable verdict by faith in Messiah's finished work and shed blood.

## 4. Petition the Courts of Heaven to Dismiss All of Satan's Charges

Heavenly Father and Righteous Judge, based upon Yeshua's finished work and my heartfelt repentance, I now move on the Court of Heaven to dismiss all of satan's accusations and charges against me and my bloodline in Jesus's name. Righteous Judge, dismiss every one of satan's accusation connected to every evil scheme of satan to bring about my premature death. For it is written in Revelation 12:10 that the accuser of the brethren has been cast down. So, I petition You, heavenly Father and Righteous Judge, to cast down all of satan's accusations against me and dismiss all of satan's charges against me, in Yeshua's name, I pray.

## 5. Declare Your Authority in Christ

Heavenly Father and Righteous Judge, in Luke 10:19 (NKJV), Yeshua said, *"Behold, I give you the authority to trample on serpents and scorpions, and over all the power of the enemy, and nothing shall by any means hurt you."* Heavenly

Father, as I prepare myself to pronounce powerful apostolic and prophetic decrees, I totally acknowledge my God-given authority in Christ to trample on serpents and scorpions that satan has weaponized against me and my destiny, in Yeshua's mighty name, I pray. The Bible also says in Proverbs 28:1 (NKJV), "*The wicked flee when no one pursues, but the righteous are bold as a lion.*" Heavenly Father because of my God-given authority in Christ, I am as bold as lion. No messenger of satan, human or demonic, can intimidate me. I am like Mount Zion, which cannot be moved, in Yeshua's mighty name, I pray. I thank You, heavenly Father, that in Mark 16:17-18, Yeshua gave me the authority to cast out devils and take up serpents and to bring God's healing power to those who are sick and oppressed. I therefore make the following decrees, completely assured of both my identity and authority in Christ Jesus!

## 6. Loudly Declare These Supernatural Decrees So You Can Have Your Breakthrough:

- Heavenly Father, I decree and declare that the power of every evil scheme of satan to bring about my premature death is completely broken over my life. I decree that I am no longer a victim of demonic technologies designed to bring about my premature death, in Yeshua's name.

- I decree and declare that You are setting me free from every evil scheme of satan to bring about my premature death that causes physical and spiritual death in Yeshua's name.

- I decree and declare that the Holy Spirit is setting me free from every evil scheme of satan to bring about my premature death that has caused any kind of spiritual blindness in my life, in Yeshua's name, I pray.

- I decree and declare that the Holy Spirit is setting me free from every evil scheme of satan to bring about my premature death would cause me not to live out all the days God apportioned for me, in Yeshua's name, I pray.

- I decree and declare that as I bring my sacrificial offering into the courts of Heaven, the power of every evil scheme of satan to bring about my premature death that satan has placed over my finances is now destroyed, in Yeshua's name.

- I decree and declare that every evil scheme of satan to bring about my premature death, which is stopping my spiritual and mental transformation according to Romans 12:1 is removed in Yeshua's mighty name!

- I decree and declare that God is setting me free from every evil scheme of satan to bring about my premature death Yeshua's name, I pray.

- I decree and declare that everything, which has been stolen from my life because of every evil scheme of satan to bring about my premature death will now be restored back to me, in Yeshua's name, I pray.

## 7. End with Thanksgiving

Heavenly Father and Righteous Judge, I thank You that the foundation of Your throne is righteousness and justice. Thank You for giving me justice against the demonic entities behind every evil scheme of satan to bring about my premature death. Heavenly Father, I thank You that because of the finished work of Yeshua on the Cross, You have translated me from the kingdom of darkness to Your glorious Kingdom of Light! Heavenly Father, since You have adopted me into your divine family, I thank You that You always hear me, when I pray. I thank You that every apostolic and prophetic decree that I have made has been heard. Thank You, Lord, that everything I have just decreed is on its way to full manifestation in Yeshua's mighty name. Heavenly Father, until the manifestation, I will maintain an aggressive attitude of thanksgiving for the complete manifestation of what I have decreed today! In Yeshua's name I pray.

# Decrees for Releasing the North Wind

Out of its chamber comes the storm, and cold from the north wind (**Job 37:9 AMP**).

For not from the east, nor from the west, nor from the desert comes exaltation. But God is the Judge; He puts down one and lifts up another (**Psalm 75:6-7 AMP**).

## Prayer of Activation

### 1. Worship God

Heavenly Father, holy is Your name and greatly to be praised. You are the Father of Light and in You is no shadow of turning. I worship and adore You in Yeshua's name, for this purpose was I created, to give You pleasure through my love and adoration. May Your Kingdom manifest in my life as it is in Heaven. Plead my cause, O Lord, with those who strive with me; fight against any entity or person who is contending against me and what is written about me in Your book of destiny. Heavenly Father, it is written in Psalm 27:6 (NASB), *"And now my head will be lifted up above my enemies around me, and I will offer sacrifices in His tent with shouts of joy; I will sing, yes, I will sing praises to the Lord."* Heavenly Father, I thank You

that I will never be swallowed by the demonic powers because You are the Lifter of my head. Abba Father, I enjoin my worship to the heavenly chorus of worship of Your holy angels and the crowd of witnesses, in Yeshua's mighty name.

## 2. Enter the Courts of Heaven

Heavenly Father, Righteous Judge, I ask that the courts of Heaven be seated according to Daniel 7:9-10 (AMP) and that all books related to my life and destiny be opened. I ask this in Yeshua's mighty name. It is written: *"I kept looking until thrones were set up, and the Ancient of Days (God) took His seat; His garment was white as snow and the hair of His head like pure wool. His throne was flames of fire; its wheels were a burning fire. A river of fire was flowing and coming out from before Him; a thousand thousands were attending Him, and ten thousand times ten thousand were standing before Him; the court was seated, and the books were opened."* Heavenly Father, Righteous Judge, I am requesting the privilege of standing before the courtroom of the Ancient of Days according to what was revealed to the prophet Daniel, in Yeshua's name, I pray. Heavenly Father, I stand in Your royal courtroom because of the shed blood and finished work of Yeshua on the Cross. I have come to receive Your righteous judgment over my life against every evil wind that satan has been using against me. Heavenly Father, Righteous Judge, I also petition You for the mobilization of the north wind on my behalf and for the advancement of Your Kingdom, in Yeshua's name! Heavenly Father, I call upon Your holy angels to be witnesses to my lawsuit and righteous prosecution of every evil wind that is working against me. I decree and declare that the power of the north wind to bring about promotion and healing rain will be released over my life, so I can achieve my God-given destiny here on earth, in Yeshua's name I pray.

## 3. Repent

Heavenly Father, Righteous Judge, it is written, *"If we confess our sins, He is faithful and just to forgive us our sins and to cleanse us from all unrighteousness"* (1 John 1:9 NKJV). I therefore activate the law of repentance and present before this court my heartfelt repentance for my personal transgressions, and for the iniquities of my forefathers that opened the door for the powers of darkness to oppress my life and bloodline, in Yeshua's name I pray. Heavenly Father, I ask that the blood of Yeshua wash away every iniquity of my forefathers that the enemy is using as a legal right to build cases against me and to bind me to every evil north wind of darkness. I also repent for all self-inflicted word curses and covenants with demons that have existed in my ancestral bloodline. I am asking that every ancestral agreement with demonic powers and evil altars will now be revoked. I petition the courts of Heaven to silence their right to claim me and my bloodline, in Yeshua's name. Thank You, Lord, for revoking these demonically engineered covenants and evil altars in Yeshua's mighty name! Heavenly Father and Righteous Judge, it is my heartfelt desire to divorce myself from every evil north wind of darkness that is operating in my life. I petition the Ancient of Days to grant me a verdict of judicial emancipation from the oppressive power of every evil north wind of darkness. I receive Your favorable verdict by faith in Messiah's finished work and shed blood.

## 4. Petition the Courts of Heaven to Dismiss All of Satan's Charges

Heavenly Father and Righteous Judge, based upon Yeshua's finished work and my heartfelt repentance, I now move on the Court of Heaven to dismiss all of satan's accusations and charges against me and my bloodline in Jesus's name. Righteous Judge, dismiss every one of satan's accusation connected to every evil north wind that is oppressing my life. For it is written in Revelation 12:10 that the accuser of the brethren has been cast down. So, I petition You Heavenly Father and Righteous Judge to cast down all of

satan's accusations against me and dismiss all of satan's charges against me, in Yeshua's name, I pray.

## 5. Declare Your Authority in Christ

Heavenly Father and Righteous Judge, in Luke 10:19 (NKJV), Yeshua says, *"Behold, I give you the authority to trample on serpents and scorpions, and over all the power of the enemy, and nothing shall by any means hurt you."* Heavenly Father, as I prepare myself to pronounce powerful apostolic and prophetic decrees, I totally acknowledge my God-given authority in Christ to trample on serpents and scorpions that satan has weaponized against me and my destiny, in Yeshua's mighty name, I pray. The Bible also says in Proverbs 28:1 (NKJV), *"The wicked flee when no one pursues, but the righteous are bold as a lion."* Heavenly Father, because of my God-given authority in Christ, I am as bold as lion. No messenger of satan, human or demonic, can intimidate me. I am like Mount Zion, which cannot be moved, in Yeshua's mighty name, I pray. I thank You, heavenly Father, that in Mark 16:17-18, Yeshua gave me the authority to cast out devils and take up serpents and to bring God's healing power to those who are sick and oppressed. I therefore make the following decrees, completely assured of both my identity and authority in Christ Jesus!

## 6. Loudly Declare These Supernatural Decrees So You Can Have Your Breakthrough:

- Heavenly Father, I decree and declare that the power of every evil north wind of darkness is completely broken over my life. I decree that I am no longer a victim of these demonic evil winds of darkness, in Yeshua's name.

- I decree and declare that the supernatural power of the north wind to bring about all manner of promotion is now released in my life, in Yeshua's name.

- I decree and declare that the Holy Spirit is setting me free from any form of witchcraft or magic originating from the north by the superior power of the north wind, in Yeshua's name, I pray.

- I decree and declare that the supernatural power of the north wind to bring about spiritual and natural rain is now released in my life, in Yeshua's name.

- I decree and declare that as I bring my sacrificial offering into the courts of Heaven, the power of every evil north wind that satan released against my finances is now destroyed, in Yeshua's name.

- I decree and declare that the supernatural power of the north wind to freeze the works of the devil, is now released in my life, in Yeshua's name.

- I decree and declare that God is setting me free from every evil north wind designed to cripple me spiritually, in Yeshua's name, I pray.

- I decree and declare that everything, which has been stolen from my life because of the power of darkness, is now being restored back to me by the operation of the north wind guided by the power of the Holy Spirit, in Yeshua's name, I pray.

## 7. End with Thanksgiving

Heavenly Father and Righteous Judge, I thank You that the foundation of Your throne is righteousness and justice. Thank You for giving me justice against the demonic entities behind any evil north wind weaponized by satan. Heavenly Father, I thank You that because of the finished work of Yeshua on the Cross, You have translated me from the kingdom of darkness to Your glorious Kingdom of Light! Heavenly Father, since You have adopted me into Your divine family, I thank You that You always hear me, when I pray. I thank You that every apostolic and prophetic decree that I have made has been heard. Thank You, Lord, that everything I have just decreed is on its way to full manifestation in Yeshua's mighty name. Heavenly Father, until the manifestation, I will maintain an aggressive attitude of thanksgiving for the complete manifestation of what I have decreed today! In Yeshua's name I pray.

# Decrees for Releasing the East Wind

Then Moses stretched out his hand over the sea; and the Lord caused the sea to go back by a strong east wind all that night, and made the sea into dry land, and the waters were divided (**Exodus 14:21 NKJV**).

## Prayer of Activation

### 1. Worship God

Heavenly Father, holy is Your name and greatly to be praised. You are the Father of Light and in You is no shadow of turning. I worship and adore You in Yeshua's name, for this purpose was I created, to give You pleasure through my love and adoration. May Your Kingdom manifest in my life as it is in Heaven. Plead my cause, O Lord, with those who strive with me; fight against any entity or person who is contending against me and what is written about me in Your book of destiny. Heavenly Father, it is written in Psalm 27:6 (NASB), *"And now my head will be lifted up above my enemies around me, and I will offer sacrifices in His tent with shouts of joy; I will sing, yes, I will sing praises to the Lord."* Heavenly Father, I thank You that I will never be swallowed by the demonic powers because You are the Lifter of my head. Abba Father, I enjoin my worship to the heavenly chorus of worship of Your holy angels and the crowd of witnesses, in Yeshua's mighty name.

## 2. Enter the Courts of Heaven

Heavenly Father, Righteous Judge, I ask that the courts of Heaven be seated according to Daniel 7:9-10 (AMP) and that all books related to my life and destiny be opened. I ask this in Yeshua's mighty name. It is written: *"I kept looking until thrones were set up, and the Ancient of Days (God) took His seat; His garment was white as snow and the hair of His head like pure wool. His throne was flames of fire; its wheels were a burning fire. A river of fire was flowing and coming out from before Him; a thousand thousands were attending Him, and ten thousand times ten thousand were standing before Him; the court was seated, and the books were opened."* Heavenly Father, Righteous Judge, I am requesting the privilege of standing before the courtroom of the Ancient of Days according to what was revealed to the prophet Daniel, in Yeshua's name, I pray. Heavenly Father, I stand in Your royal courtroom because of the shed blood and finished work of Yeshua on the Cross. I have come to receive Your righteous judgment over my life against every evil east wind that satan has been using against me. Heavenly Father, Righteous Judge, I also petition You for the mobilization of the east wind on my behalf and for the advancement of Your Kingdom, in Yeshua's name! Heavenly Father, I call upon Your holy angels to be witnesses to my lawsuit and righteous prosecution of every evil wind that is working against me. I decree and declare that the power of the east wind to bring about the judgments of God against all works of wickedness is released against every plan of satan against me, so I can achieve my God-given destiny here on earth, in Yeshua's name I pray.

## 3. Repent

Heavenly Father, Righteous Judge, it is written, *"If we confess our sins, He is faithful and just to forgive us our sins and to cleanse us from all unrighteousness"*

(1 John 1:9 NKJV). I therefore activate the law of repentance and present before this court my heartfelt repentance for my personal transgressions, and for the iniquities of my forefathers that opened the door for the powers of darkness to oppress my life and bloodline, in Yeshua's name I pray. Heavenly Father, I ask that the blood of Yeshua wash away every iniquity of my forefathers that the enemy is using as a legal right to build cases against me and to bind me to every evil east wind of darkness. I also repent for all self-inflicted word curses and covenants with demons that have existed in my ancestral bloodline. I am asking that every ancestral agreement with demonic powers and evil altars will now be revoked. I petition the courts of Heaven to silence their right to claim me and my bloodline, in Yeshua's name. Thank You, Lord, for revoking these demonically engineered covenants and evil altars in Yeshua's mighty name! Heavenly Father and Righteous Judge, it is my heartfelt desire to divorce myself from every evil east wind of darkness that is operating in my life. I petition the Ancient of Days to grant me a verdict of judicial emancipation from the oppressive power of every evil east wind of darkness. I receive Your favorable verdict by faith in Messiah's finished work and shed blood.

## 4. Petition the Courts of Heaven to Dismiss All of Satan's Charges

Heavenly Father and Righteous Judge, based upon Yeshua's finished work and my heartfelt repentance, I now move on the court of Heaven to dismiss all of satan's accusations and charges against me and my bloodline in Jesus's name. Righteous Judge, dismiss every one of satan's accusation connected to every evil east wind that is oppressing my life. For it is written in Revelation 12:10 that the accuser of the brethren has been cast down. So, I petition You, heavenly Father and Righteous Judge, to cast down all of satan's accusations against me and dismiss all of satan's charges against me, in Yeshua's name, I pray.

## 5. Declare Your Authority in Christ

Heavenly Father and Righteous Judge, in Luke 10:19 (NKJV), Yeshua says, *"Behold, I give you the authority to trample on serpents and scorpions, and over all the power of the enemy, and nothing shall by any means hurt you."* Heavenly Father, as I prepare myself to pronounce powerful apostolic and prophetic decrees, I totally acknowledge my God-given authority in Christ to trample on serpents and scorpions that satan has weaponized against me and my destiny, in Yeshua's mighty name, I pray. The Bible also says in Proverbs 28:1 (NKJV), *"The wicked flee when no one pursues, but the righteous are bold as a lion."* Heavenly Father because of my God-given authority in Christ, I am as bold as lion. No messenger of satan, human or demonic, can intimidate me. I am like Mount Zion, which cannot be moved, in Yeshua's mighty name, I pray. I thank You, heavenly Father that in Mark 16:17-18, Yeshua gave me the authority to cast out devils and take up serpents and to bring God's healing power to those who are sick and oppressed. I therefore make the following decrees, completely assured of both my identity and authority in Christ Jesus!

## 6. Loudly Declare These Supernatural Decrees So You Can Have Your Breakthrough:

- Heavenly Father, I decree and declare that the power of every evil east wind of darkness is completely broken over my life. I decree that I am no longer a victim of these demonic evil wind of darkness, in Yeshua's name.

- I decree and declare that the supernatural power of the east wind to judge the works of darkness is in now released in my life, in Yeshua's name.

- I decree and declare that the Holy Spirit is setting me free from any form of witchcraft or magic originating from the east by the superior power of the east wind, in Yeshua's name, I pray.

- I decree and declare that the supernatural power of the east wind to tear down demonic strongholds is now released in my life, in Yeshua's name.

- I decree and declare that as I bring my sacrificial offering into the courts of Heaven, the power of every evil east wind that satan released against my finances is now destroyed, in Yeshua's name.

- I decree and declare that the supernatural power of the east wind to fight against whatever the enemy has secretly planted in my body, house, business, or workplace, is now released in my life, in Yeshua's name.

- I decree and declare that God is setting me free from every evil east wind designed me cripple me spiritually, in Yeshua's name, I pray.

- I decree and declare that everything, which has been stolen from my life because of the power of darkness, is now being restored back to me by the operation of the east wind guided by the power of the Holy Spirit, in Yeshua's name, I pray.

## 7. End with Thanksgiving

Heavenly Father and Righteous Judge, I thank You that the foundation of Your throne is righteousness and justice. Thank You for giving me justice against the demonic entities behind any evil east wind, weaponized by satan.

Heavenly Father, I thank You that because of the finished work of Yeshua on the Cross, You have translated me from the kingdom of darkness to Your glorious Kingdom of Light! Heavenly Father, since You have adopted me into Your divine family, I thank You that You always hear me, when I pray. I thank You that every apostolic and prophetic decree that I have made has been heard. Thank You, Lord, that everything I have just decreed is on its way to full manifestation in Yeshua's mighty name. Heavenly Father, until the manifestation, I will maintain an aggressive attitude of thanksgiving for the complete manifestation of what I have decreed today! In Yeshua's name I pray.

# Decrees for Releasing the West Wind

So he went out from Pharaoh and entreated the Lord. And the Lord turned a very strong west wind, which took the locusts away and blew them into the Red Sea. There remained not one locust in all the territory of Egypt (**Exodus 10:18-19 NKJV**).

## Prayer of Activation

### 1. Worship God

Heavenly Father, holy is Your name and greatly to be praised. You are the Father of Light and in You is no shadow of turning. I worship and adore You in Yeshua's name, for this purpose was I created, to give You pleasure through my love and adoration. May Your Kingdom manifest in my life as it is in Heaven. Plead my cause, O Lord, with those who strive with me; fight against any entity or person who is contending against me and what is written about me in Your book of destiny. Heavenly Father, it is written in Psalm 27:6 (NASB), *"And now my head will be lifted up above my enemies around me, and I will offer sacrifices in His tent with shouts of joy; I will sing, yes, I will sing praises to the Lord."* Heavenly Father, I thank You that I will never be swallowed by the demonic powers because You are the Lifter of my head. Abba Father, I enjoin my worship to the heavenly chorus of

worship of Your holy angels and the crowd of witnesses, in Yeshua's mighty name.

## 2. Enter the Courts of Heaven

Heavenly Father, Righteous Judge, I ask that the courts of Heaven be seated according to Daniel 7:9-10 (AMP) and that all books related to my life and destiny be opened. I ask this in Yeshua's mighty name. It is written: *"I kept looking until thrones were set up, and the Ancient of Days (God) took His seat; His garment was white as snow and the hair of His head like pure wool. His throne was flames of fire; its wheels were a burning fire. A river of fire was flowing and coming out from before Him; a thousand thousands were attending Him, and ten thousand times ten thousand were standing before Him; the court was seated, and the books were opened."* Heavenly Father, Righteous Judge, I am requesting the privilege of standing before the courtroom of the Ancient of Days according to what was revealed to the prophet Daniel, in Yeshua's name, I pray. Heavenly Father, I stand in Your royal courtroom because of the shed blood and finished work of Yeshua on the Cross. I have come to receive Your righteous judgment over my life against every evil west wind that satan has been using against me. Heavenly Father, Righteous Judge, I also petition You for the mobilization of the west wind on my behalf and for the advancement of Your Kingdom, in Yeshua's name! Heavenly Father, I call upon Your holy angels to be witnesses to my lawsuit and righteous prosecution of every evil wind that is working against me. I decree and declare that the power of the west wind to bring about divine refreshment and restoration is now released over my life, so I can achieve my God-given destiny here on earth, in Yeshua's name I pray.

## 3. Repent

Heavenly Father, Righteous Judge, it is written, *"If we confess our sins, He is faithful and just to forgive us our sins and to cleanse us from all unrighteousness"*

(1 John 1:9 NKJV). I therefore activate the law of repentance and present before this court my heartfelt repentance for my personal transgressions, and for the iniquities of my forefathers that opened the door for the powers of darkness to oppress my life and bloodline, in Yeshua's name I pray. Heavenly Father, I ask that the blood of Yeshua wash away every iniquity of my forefathers that the enemy is using as a legal right to build cases against me and to bind me to every evil west wind of darkness. I also repent for all self-inflicted word curses and covenants with demons that have existed in my ancestral bloodline. I am asking that every ancestral agreement with demonic powers and evil altars will now be revoked. I petition the courts of Heaven to silence their right to claim me and my bloodline, in Yeshua's name. Thank You, Lord, for revoking these demonically engineered covenants and evil altars in Yeshua's mighty name! Heavenly Father and Righteous Judge, it is my heartfelt desire to divorce myself from every evil west wind of darkness that is operating in my life. I petition the Ancient of Days to grant me a verdict of judicial emancipation from the oppressive power of every evil west wind of darkness. I receive Your favorable verdict by faith in Messiah's finished work and shed blood.

## 4. Petition the Courts of Heaven to Dismiss All of Satan's Charges

Heavenly Father and Righteous Judge, based upon Yeshua's finished work and my heartfelt repentance, I now move on the court of Heaven to dismiss all of satan's accusations and charges against me and my bloodline in Jesus's name. Righteous Judge, dismiss every one of satan's accusation connected to every evil west wind that is oppressing my life. For it is written in Revelation 12:10 that the accuser of the brethren has been cast down. So, I petition You, heavenly Father and Righteous Judge, to cast down all of satan's accusations against me and dismiss all of satan's charges against me, in Yeshua's name, I pray.

## 5. Declare Your Authority in Christ

Heavenly Father and Righteous Judge, in Luke 10:19 (NKJV), Yeshua says, *"Behold, I give you the authority to trample on serpents and scorpions, and over all the power of the enemy, and nothing shall by any means hurt you."* Heavenly Father, as I prepare myself to pronounce powerful apostolic and prophetic decrees, I totally acknowledge my God-given authority in Christ to trample on serpents and scorpions that satan has weaponized against me and my destiny, in Yeshua's mighty name, I pray. The Bible also says in Proverbs 28:1 (NKJV), *"The wicked flee when no one pursues, but the righteous are bold as a lion."* Heavenly Father, because of my God-given authority in Christ, I am as bold as lion. No messenger of satan, human or demonic, can intimidate me. I am like Mount Zion, which cannot be moved, in Yeshua's mighty name, I pray. I thank You, heavenly Father, that in Mark 16:17-18, Yeshua gave me the authority to cast out devils and take up serpents and to bring God's healing power to those who are sick and oppressed. I therefore make the following decrees, completely assured of both my identity and authority in Christ Jesus!

## 6. Loudly Declare These Supernatural Decrees So You Can Have Your Breakthrough:

- Heavenly Father, I decree and declare that the power of every evil west wind of darkness is completely broken over my life. I decree that I am no longer a victim of these demonic evil wind of darkness, in Yeshua's name.

- I decree and declare that the supernatural power of the west wind to bring about divine refreshment is now released in my life, in Yeshua's name.

- I decree and declare that the Holy Spirit is setting me free from any form of witchcraft or magic originating from the west by the superior power of the north wind, in Yeshua's name, I pray.

- I decree and declare that the supernatural power of the west wind to bring about spiritual and natural restoration is now released in my life, in Yeshua's name.

- I decree and declare that as I bring my sacrificial offering into the courts of Heaven, the power of every evil west wind that satan released against my finances is now destroyed, in Yeshua's name.

- I decree and declare that the supernatural power of the west wind to overthrow the works of the devil, is now released in my life, in Yeshua's name.

- I decree and declare that God is setting me free from every evil west wind, designed me cripple me spiritually, in Yeshua's name, I pray.

- I decree and declare that everything, which has been stolen from my life because of the power of darkness, is now being restored back to me by the operation of the west wind guided by the power of the Holy Spirit, in Yeshua's name, I pray.

## 7. End with Thanksgiving

Heavenly Father and Righteous Judge, I thank You that the foundation of Your throne is righteousness and justice. Thank You for giving me justice against the demonic entities behind any evil west wind, weaponized by satan. Heavenly Father, I thank You that because of the finished work of Yeshua on the Cross, You have translated me from the kingdom of darkness to Your glorious Kingdom of Light! Heavenly Father, since You have adopted me into Your divine family, I thank You that You always hear me, when I pray. I thank You that every apostolic and prophetic decree that I have made has been heard. Thank You, Lord, that everything I have just decreed is on its way to full manifestation in Yeshua's mighty name. Heavenly Father, until the manifestation, I will maintain an aggressive attitude of thanksgiving for the complete manifestation of what I have decreed today! In Yeshua's name I pray.

# Decrees for Releasing the South Wind

The burden against the Wilderness of the Sea. As whirlwinds in the South pass through, so it comes from the desert, from a terrible land (**Isaiah 21:1 NKJV**).

From the chamber of the south comes the whirlwind, and cold from the scattering winds of the north (**Job 37:9 NKJV**).

## Prayer of Activation

### 1. Worship God

Heavenly Father, holy is Your name and greatly to be praised. You are the Father of Light and in You is no shadow of turning. I worship and adore You in Yeshua's name, for this purpose was I created, to give You pleasure through my love and adoration. May Your Kingdom manifest in my life as it is in Heaven. Plead my cause, O Lord, with those who strive with me; fight against any entity or person who is contending against me and what is written about me in Your book of destiny. Heavenly Father, it is written in Psalm 27:6 (NASB), *"And now my head will be lifted up above my enemies around me, and I will offer sacrifices in His tent with shouts of joy; I will sing, yes, I will sing praises to the Lord."* Heavenly Father, I thank You

that I will never be swallowed by the demonic powers because You are the Lifter of my head. Abba Father, I enjoin my worship to the heavenly chorus of worship of Your holy angels and the crowd of witnesses, in Yeshua's mighty name.

## 2. Enter the Courts of Heaven

Heavenly Father, Righteous Judge, I ask that the courts of Heaven be seated according to Daniel 7:9-10 (AMP) and that all books related to my life and destiny be opened. I ask this in Yeshua's mighty name. It is written: *"I kept looking until thrones were set up, and the Ancient of Days (God) took His seat; His garment was white as snow and the hair of His head like pure wool. His throne was flames of fire; its wheels were a burning fire. A river of fire was flowing and coming out from before Him; a thousand thousands were attending Him, and ten thousand times ten thousand were standing before Him; the court was seated, and the books were opened."* Heavenly Father, Righteous Judge, I am requesting the privilege of standing before the courtroom of the Ancient of Days according to what was revealed to the prophet Daniel, in Yeshua's name, I pray. Heavenly Father, I stand in Your royal courtroom because of the shed blood and finished work of Yeshua on the Cross. I have come to receive Your righteous judgment over my life against every evil south wind that satan has been using against me. Heavenly Father, Righteous Judge, I also petition You for the mobilization of the south wind on my behalf and for the advancement of Your Kingdom, in Yeshua's name! Heavenly Father, I call upon Your holy angels to be witnesses to my lawsuit and righteous prosecution of every evil wind that is working against me. I decree and declare that the power of the south wind to bring about the supernatural power of God according to Nahum 1:3, is now released over my life, so I can achieve my God-given destiny here on earth, in Yeshua's name I pray.

## 3. Repent

Heavenly Father, Righteous Judge, it is written, *"If we confess our sins, He is faithful and just to forgive us our sins and to cleanse us from all unrighteousness"* (1 John 1:9 NKJV). I therefore activate the law of repentance and present before this court my heartfelt repentance for my personal transgressions, and for the iniquities of my forefathers that opened the door for the powers of darkness to oppress my life and bloodline, in Yeshua's name I pray. Heavenly Father, I ask that the blood of Yeshua wash away every iniquity of my forefathers that the enemy is using as a legal right to build cases against me and to bind me to every evil south wind of darkness. I also repent for all self-inflicted word curses and covenants with demons that have existed in my ancestral bloodline. I am asking that every ancestral agreement with demonic powers and evil altars will now be revoked. I petition the courts of Heaven to silence their right to claim me and my bloodline, in Yeshua's name. Thank You, Lord, for revoking these demonically engineered covenants and evil altars in Yeshua's mighty name! Heavenly Father and Righteous Judge, it is my heartfelt desire to divorce myself from every evil south wind of darkness that is operating in my life. I petition the Ancient of Days to grant me a verdict of judicial emancipation from the oppressive power of every evil south wind of darkness. I receive Your favorable verdict by faith in Messiah's finished work and shed blood.

## 4. Petition the Courts of Heaven to Dismiss All of Satan's Charges

Heavenly Father and Righteous Judge, based upon Yeshua's finished work and my heartfelt repentance, I now move on the court of Heaven to dismiss all of satan's accusations and charges against me and my bloodline in Jesus's name. Righteous Judge, dismiss every one of satan's accusation connected to every evil south wind that is oppressing my life. For it is written in Revelation 12:10 that the accuser of the brethren has been cast down. So, I petition You, heavenly Father and Righteous Judge, to cast down all of

satan's accusations against me and dismiss all of satan's charges against me, in Yeshua's name, I pray.

## 5. Declare Your Authority in Christ

Heavenly Father and Righteous Judge, in Luke 10:19 (NKJV), Yeshua says, *"Behold, I give you the authority to trample on serpents and scorpions, and over all the power of the enemy, and nothing shall by any means hurt you."* Heavenly Father, as I prepare myself to pronounce powerful apostolic and prophetic decrees, I totally acknowledge my God-given authority in Christ to trample on serpents and scorpions that satan has weaponized against me and my destiny, in Yeshua's mighty name, I pray. The Bible also says in Proverbs 28:1 (NKJV), *"The wicked flee when no one pursues, but the righteous are bold as a lion."* Heavenly Father, because of my God-given authority in Christ, I am as bold as lion. No messenger of satan, human or demonic, can intimidate me. I am like Mount Zion, which cannot be moved, in Yeshua's mighty name, I pray. I thank You, Heavenly Father, that in Mark 16:17-18, Yeshua gave me the authority to cast out devils and take up serpents and to bring God's healing power to those who are sick and oppressed. I therefore make the following decrees, completely assured of both my identity and authority in Christ Jesus!

## 6. Loudly Declare These Supernatural Decrees So You Can Have Your Breakthrough:

- Heavenly Father, I decree and declare that the power of every evil south wind of darkness is completely broken over my life. I decree that I am no longer a victim of these demonic evil wind of darkness, in Yeshua's name.

- I decree and declare that the supernatural power of the south wind to bring about the power of God is now released in my life, in Yeshua's name.

- I decree and declare that the Holy Spirit is setting me free from any form of witchcraft or magic originating from the south by the superior power of the south wind, in Yeshua's name, I pray.

- I decree and declare that the supernatural power of the south wind to bring about spiritual and natural ascendancy is now released in my life, in Yeshua's name.

- I decree and declare that as I bring my sacrificial offering into the courts of Heaven, the power of every evil south wind that satan released against my finances is now destroyed, in Yeshua's name.

- I decree and declare that the supernatural power of the south wind to judge and destroy the works of the devil, is now released in my life, in Yeshua's name.

- I decree and declare that God is setting me free from every evil south wind, designed me cripple me spiritually, in Yeshua's name, I pray.

- I decree and declare that everything, which has been stolen from my life because of the power of darkness, is now being restored back to me by the operation of the south wind where God's power is hidden, in Yeshua's name, I pray.

## 7. End with Thanksgiving

Heavenly Father and Righteous Judge, I thank You that the foundation of Your throne is righteousness and justice. Thank You for giving me justice against the demonic entities behind any evil south wind, weaponized by satan. Heavenly Father, I thank You that because of the finished work of Yeshua on the Cross, You have translated me from the kingdom of darkness to Your glorious Kingdom of Light! Heavenly Father, since You have adopted me into Your divine family, I thank You that You always hear me, when I pray. I thank You that every apostolic and prophetic decree that I have made has been heard. Thank You, Lord, that everything I have just decreed is on its way to full manifestation in Yeshua's mighty name. Heavenly Father, until the manifestation, I will maintain an aggressive attitude of thanksgiving for the complete manifestation of what I have decreed today! In Yeshua's name I pray.

# Decrees for Releasing Angelic Intervention

For He shall give His angels charge over you, to keep you in all your ways. In their hands they shall bear you up, lest you dash your foot against a stone. You shall tread upon the lion and the cobra, the young lion and the serpent you shall trample underfoot (**Psalm 91:11-13 NKJV**).

## Prayer of Activation

### 1. Worship God

Heavenly Father, holy is Your name and greatly to be praised. You are the Father of Light and in You is no shadow of turning. I worship and adore You in Yeshua's name, for this purpose was I created, to give You pleasure through my love and adoration. May Your Kingdom manifest in my life as it is in Heaven. Plead my cause, O Lord, with those who strive with me; fight against any entity or person who is contending against me and what is written about me in Your book of destiny. Heavenly Father, it is written in Psalm 27:6 (NASB), *"And now my head will be lifted up above my enemies around me, and I will offer sacrifices in His tent with shouts of joy;*

*I will sing, yes, I will sing praises to the Lord."* Heavenly Father, I thank You that I will never be swallowed by the demonic powers because You are the Lifter of my head. Abba Father, I enjoin my worship to the heavenly chorus of worship of Your holy angels and the crowd of witnesses, in Yeshua's mighty name.

## 2. Enter the Courts of Heaven

Heavenly Father, Righteous Judge, I ask that the courts of Heaven be seated according to Daniel 7:9-10 (AMP) and that all books related to my life and destiny be opened. I ask this in Yeshua's mighty name. It is written: *"I kept looking until thrones were set up, and the Ancient of Days (God) took His seat; His garment was white as snow and the hair of His head like pure wool. His throne was flames of fire; its wheels were a burning fire. A river of fire was flowing and coming out from before Him; a thousand thousands were attending Him, and ten thousand times ten thousand were standing before Him; the court was seated, and the books were opened."* Heavenly Father, Righteous Judge, I am requesting the privilege of standing before the courtroom of the Ancient of Days according to what was revealed to the prophet Daniel, in Yeshua's name, I pray. Heavenly Father, I stand in Your royal courtroom because of the shed blood and finished work of Yeshua on the Cross. I have come to receive Your righteous judgment over my life against every work of satan that he has been using against me. Heavenly Father, Righteous Judge I make a petition for the release of warring angels on my behalf, so I can achieve my God-given destiny here on earth, in Yeshua's name I pray.

## 3. Repent

Heavenly Father, Righteous Judge, it is written, *"If we confess our sins, He is faithful and just to forgive us our sins and to cleanse us from all unrighteousness"* (1 John 1:9 NKJV). I therefore activate the law of repentance and present before this court my heartfelt repentance for my personal transgressions, and for the iniquities of my forefathers that opened the door for every work of darkness to oppress my life and bloodline, in Yeshua's name I pray. Heavenly Father, I ask that the blood of Yeshua wash away every iniquity of my forefathers that the enemy is using as a legal right to build cases against me and to bind me to every evil veil of darkness. I also repent for all self-inflicted word curses and covenants with demons that have existed in my ancestral bloodline. I am asking that every ancestral agreement with demonic powers and evil altars will now be revoked. I petition the courts of Heaven to silence their right to claim me and my bloodline, in Yeshua's name. Thank You, Lord, for revoking these demonically engineered covenants and evil altars in Yeshua's mighty name! Heavenly Father and Righteous Judge, it is my heartfelt desire to divorce myself from every power of darkness that is operating in my life. I petition the Ancient of Days to grant me a verdict of judicial emancipation from the oppressive power of every power of darkness through the ministry of the angel armies. I receive Your favorable verdict by faith in Messiah's finished work and shed blood.

## 4. Petition the Courts of Heaven to Dismiss All of Satan's Charges

Heavenly Father and Righteous Judge, based upon Yeshua's finished work and my heartfelt repentance, I now move on the court of Heaven to dismiss all of satan's accusations and charges against me and my bloodline in Jesus's name. Righteous Judge, dismiss every one of satan's accusation that is hindering the manifestation of my destiny. For it is written in Revelation 12:10 that the accuser of the brethren has been cast down. So, I petition You, heavenly Father and Righteous Judge, to cast down all of satan's accusations against me and dismiss all of satan's charges against me, in Yeshua's name, I pray.

## 5. Declare Your Authority in Christ

Heavenly Father and Righteous Judge, in Luke 10:19 (NKJV), Yeshua says, *"Behold, I give you the authority to trample on serpents and scorpions, and over all the power of the enemy, and nothing shall by any means hurt you."* Heavenly Father, as I prepare myself to pronounce powerful apostolic and prophetic decrees, I totally acknowledge my God-given authority in Christ to trample on serpents and scorpions that satan has weaponized against me and my destiny, in Yeshua's mighty name, I pray. The Bible also says in Proverbs 28:1 (NKJV), *"The wicked flee when no one pursues, but the righteous are bold as a lion."* Heavenly Father, because of my God-given authority in Christ, I am as bold as lion. No messenger of satan, human or demonic, can intimidate me. I am like Mount Zion, which cannot be moved, in Yeshua's mighty name, I pray. I thank You, heavenly Father, that in Mark 16:17-18, Yeshua gave me the authority to cast out devils and take up serpents and to bring God's healing power to those who are sick and oppressed. I therefore make the following decrees, completely assured of both my identity and authority in Christ Jesus!

## 6. Loudly Declare These Supernatural Decrees So You Can Have Your Breakthrough:

- Heavenly Father I decree and declare that through the operation of the angel army, the power of darkness is completely broken over my life. I decree that I am no longer a victim of satan's scheming, in Yeshua's name.

- I decree and declare that you are releasing angels to fight for my God-given destiny, in Yeshua's name.

- I decree and declare that angels are setting me free from any form of witchcraft or magic that was weaponized against me, in Yeshua's name, I pray.

- I decree and declare that my home and business are surrounded by a battalion of angels with flaming swords of fire, in Yeshua's name, I pray.

- I decree and declare that as I bring my sacrificial offering into the courts of Heaven, the power of the angel armies is released over my finances, in Yeshua's name.

- I decree and declare that due to the high-level activity of angels in my life, my foot will not be dashed against a stone, in Yeshua's mighty name!

- I decree and declare that angels are setting me free from every evil veil, which has caused me to be spiritually crippled in Yeshua's name, I pray.

- I decree and declare that everything, which has been stolen from my life by the powers of darkness, is being restored back to me, in Yeshua's name, I pray.

## 7. End with Thanksgiving

Heavenly Father and Righteous Judge, I thank You that the foundation of Your throne is righteousness and justice. Thank You for releasing angel armies to war for my safety and destiny. Heavenly Father, I thank You that because of the finished work of Yeshua on the Cross, You have translated me from the kingdom of darkness to Your glorious Kingdom of Light! Heavenly Father, since You have adopted me into Your divine family, I thank You that You always hear me, when I pray. I thank You that every apostolic and prophetic decree that I have made has been heard. Thank You, Lord, that everything I have just decreed is on its way to full manifestation in Yeshua's mighty name. Heavenly Father, until the manifestation, I will maintain an aggressive attitude of thanksgiving for the complete manifestation of what I have decreed today! In Yeshua's name I pray.

# Decrees for Opening the Books of Destiny

I watched till thrones were put in place, and the Ancient of Days was seated; His garment was white as snow, and the hair of His head was like pure wool. His throne was a fiery flame, Its wheels a burning fire; a fiery stream issued and came forth from before Him. A thousand thousands ministered to Him; ten thousand times ten thousand stood before Him. The court was seated, and the books were opened (Daniel 7:9-10 NKJV).

## Prayer of Activation

### 1. Worship God

Heavenly Father, holy is Your name and greatly to be praised. You are the Father of Light and in You is no shadow of turning. I worship and adore You in Yeshua's name, for this purpose was I created, to give You pleasure through my love and adoration. May Your Kingdom manifest in my life as it is in Heaven. Plead my cause, O Lord, with those who strive with me; fight against any entity or person who is contending against me and what is written about me in Your book of destiny. Heavenly Father,

it is written in Psalm 27:6 (NASB), *"And now my head will be lifted up above my enemies around me, and I will offer sacrifices in His tent with shouts of joy; I will sing, yes, I will sing praises to the Lord."* Heavenly Father, I thank You that I will never be swallowed by the demonic powers because You are the Lifter of my head. Abba Father, I enjoin my worship to the heavenly chorus of worship of Your holy angels and the crowd of witnesses, in Yeshua's mighty name.

## 2. Enter the Courts of Heaven

Heavenly Father, Righteous Judge, I ask that the courts of Heaven be seated according to Daniel 7:9-10 (AMP) and that all books related to my life and destiny be opened. I ask this in Yeshua's mighty name. It is written: *"I kept looking until thrones were set up, and the Ancient of Days (God) took His seat; His garment was white as snow and the hair of His head like pure wool. His throne was flames of fire; its wheels were a burning fire. A river of fire was flowing and coming out from before Him; a thousand thousands were attending Him, and ten thousand times ten thousand were standing before Him; the court was seated, and the books were opened."* Heavenly Father, Righteous Judge, I am requesting the privilege of standing before the courtroom of the Ancient of Days according to what was revealed to the prophet Daniel, in Yeshua's name, I pray. Heavenly Father, I stand in Your royal courtroom because of the shed blood and finished work of Yeshua on the Cross. I have come to receive Your righteous judgment over my life against every evil scheme of satan that is contending against the opening of my books of destiny. Heavenly Father, I call upon Your holy angels to be witnesses to my lawsuit and righteous prosecution of evil scheme of satan that is contending against the opening of my books of destiny. I decree and declare that every evil scheme of satan that is contending against the opening of my books of destiny will be removed so I can achieve my God-given destiny here on earth, in Yeshua's name I pray.

## 3. Repent

Heavenly Father, Righteous Judge, it is written, *"If we confess our sins, He is faithful and just to forgive us our sins and to cleanse us from all unrighteousness"* (1 John 1:9 NKJV). I therefore activate the law of repentance and present before this court my heartfelt repentance for my personal transgressions, and for the iniquities of my forefathers that opened the door for every evil scheme of satan that is contending against the opening of my books of destiny, in Yeshua's name I pray. Heavenly Father, I ask that the blood of Yeshua wash away every iniquity of my forefathers that the enemy is using as a legal right to build cases against me that are contending against the opening of my books of destiny. I also repent for all self-inflicted word curses and covenants with demons that have existed in my ancestral bloodline. I am asking that every ancestral agreement with demonic powers and evil altars will now be revoked. I petition the courts of Heaven to silence their right to claim me and my bloodline, in Yeshua's name. Thank You, Lord, for revoking these demonically engineered covenants and evil altars in Yeshua's mighty name! Heavenly Father and Righteous Judge, it is my heartfelt desire to divorce myself from every evil scheme of satan that is contending against the opening of my books of destiny. I petition the Ancient of Days to grant me a verdict of judicial emancipation from the oppressive power of every evil scheme of satan that is contending against the opening of my books of destiny. I receive Your favorable verdict by faith in Messiah's finished work and shed blood.

## 4. Petition the Courts of Heaven to Dismiss All of Satan's Charges

Heavenly Father and Righteous Judge, based upon Yeshua's finished work and my heartfelt repentance, I now move on the court of Heaven to dismiss all of satan's accusations and charges against me and my bloodline in Jesus's name. Righteous Judge, dismiss every one of satan's accusation connected to every evil scheme of satan that is contending against the opening of my books of destiny. For it is written in Revelation 12:10 that the accuser of the brethren has been cast down. So, I petition You, heavenly Father and Righteous Judge, to cast down all of satan's accusations against me and dismiss all of satan's charges against me, in Yeshua's name, I pray.

## 5. Declare Your Authority in Christ

Heavenly Father and Righteous Judge, in Luke 10:19 (NKJV), Yeshua says, *"Behold, I give you the authority to trample on serpents and scorpions, and over all the power of the enemy, and nothing shall by any means hurt you."* Heavenly Father, as I prepare myself to pronounce powerful apostolic and prophetic decrees, I totally acknowledge my God-given authority in Christ to trample on serpents and scorpions that satan has weaponized against me and my destiny, in Yeshua's mighty name, I pray. The Bible also says in Proverbs 28:1 (NKJV), *"The wicked flee when no one pursues, but the righteous are bold as a lion."* Heavenly Father, because of my God-given authority in Christ, I am as bold as lion. No messenger of satan, human or demonic, can intimidate me. I am like Mount Zion, which cannot be moved, in Yeshua's mighty name, I pray. I thank You, heavenly Father, that in Mark 16:17-18, Yeshua gave me the authority to cast out devils and take up serpents and to bring God's healing power to those who are sick and oppressed. I therefore make the following decrees, completely assured of both my identity and authority in Christ Jesus!

## 6. Loudly Declare These Supernatural Decrees So You Can Have Your Breakthrough:

- Heavenly Father I decree and declare that the power of every evil scheme of satan that is contending against the opening of my books of destiny is completely broken over my life. I decree that I am no longer a victim of these demonic strategies, in Yeshua's name.

- I decree and declare that the Holy Spirit is opening all the books related to my God-given destiny, in Yeshua's name.

- I decree and declare that the Holy Spirit is setting me free from any operation of witchcraft or magic that is contending against the opening of my books of destiny, in Yeshua's name, I pray.

- I decree and declare that the Holy Spirit is setting me free from every veil of deception that is contending against the opening of my books of destiny, in Yeshua's name, I pray.

- I decree and declare that as I bring my sacrificial offering into the courts of Heaven, the all the finances written in my books of destiny is now released, in Yeshua's name.

- I decree and declare that every evil veil of darkness covering my books of destiny, which is stopping my spiritual and mental transformation according to Romans 12:1 is now removed in Yeshua's mighty name!

- I decree and declare that God is setting me free from every evil scheme of satan that is contending against the opening of my books of destiny, which has caused me to be spiritually crippled in Yeshua's name, I pray.

- I decree and declare that everything, which has been stolen from my life because of the power of darkness, is now restored back to me, as the Holy Spirit restores what is written about me, in Yeshua's name, I pray.

## 7. End with Thanksgiving

Heavenly Father and Righteous Judge, I thank You that the foundation of Your throne is righteousness and justice. Thank You for giving me justice against the demonic entities behind that are contending against the opening of my books of destiny. Heavenly Father, I thank You that because of the finished work of Yeshua on the Cross, You have translated me from the kingdom of darkness to Your glorious Kingdom of Light! Heavenly Father, since You have adopted me into Your divine family, I thank You that You always hear me, when I pray. I thank You that every apostolic and prophetic decree that I have made has been heard. Thank You, Lord, that everything I have just decreed is on its way to full manifestation in Yeshua's mighty name. Heavenly Father, until the manifestation, I will maintain an aggressive attitude of thanksgiving for the complete manifestation of what I have decreed today! In Yeshua's name I pray.

# Decrees for Releasing Healing

Surely He has borne our griefs and carried our sorrows; yet we esteemed Him stricken, smitten by God, and afflicted. But He was wounded for our transgressions, He was bruised for our iniquities; The chastisement for our peace was upon Him, and by His stripes we are healed (**Isaiah 53:4-5 NKJV**).

## Prayer of Activation

### 1. Worship God

Heavenly Father, holy is Your name and greatly to be praised. You are the Father of Light and in You is no shadow of turning. I worship and adore You in Yeshua's name, for this purpose was I created, to give You pleasure through my love and adoration. May Your Kingdom manifest in my life as it is in Heaven. Plead my cause, O Lord, with those who strive with me; fight against any entity or person who is contending against me and what is written about me in Your book of destiny. Heavenly Father, it is written in Psalm 27:6 (NASB), *"And now my head will be lifted up above my enemies around me, and I will offer sacrifices in His tent with shouts of joy; I will sing, yes, I will sing praises to the Lord."* Heavenly Father, I thank You that I will never be swallowed by the demonic powers because You are the

Lifter of my head. Abba Father, I enjoin my worship to the heavenly chorus of worship of Your holy angels and the crowd of witnesses, in Yeshua's mighty name.

## 2. Enter the Courts of Heaven

Heavenly Father, Righteous Judge, I ask that the Courts of Heaven be seated according to Daniel 7:9-10 (AMP) and that all books related to my life and destiny be opened. I ask this in Yeshua's mighty name. It is written: *"I kept looking until thrones were set up, and the Ancient of Days (God) took His seat; His garment was white as snow and the hair of His head like pure wool. His throne was flames of fire; its wheels were a burning fire. A river of fire was flowing and coming out from before Him; a thousand thousands were attending Him, and ten thousand times ten thousand were standing before Him; the court was seated, and the books were opened."* Heavenly Father, Righteous Judge, I am requesting the privilege of standing before the courtroom of the Ancient of Days according to what was revealed to the prophet Daniel, in Yeshua's name, I pray. Heavenly Father, I stand in Your royal courtroom because of the shed blood and finished work of Yeshua on the Cross. I have come to receive Your righteous judgment over my life against every form of sickness and disease that satan is weaponizing against me. Heavenly Father, I call upon Your holy angels to be witnesses to my lawsuit and righteous prosecution of every form of sickness and disease that satan is weaponizing against me. I decree and declare that every sickness and disease afflicting my spirit, soul, and body will be removed so I can achieve my God-given destiny here on earth, in Yeshua's name I pray.

## 3. Repent

Heavenly Father, Righteous Judge, it is written, *"If we confess our sins, He is faithful and just to forgive us our sins and to cleanse us from all unrighteousness"* (1 John 1:9 NKJV). I therefore activate the law of repentance and present

before this court my heartfelt repentance for my personal transgressions, and for the iniquities of my forefathers that opened the door for every form of sickness and disease that satan is using to oppress my life and bloodline, in Yeshua's name I pray. Heavenly Father, I ask that the blood of Yeshua wash away every iniquity of my forefathers that the enemy is using as a legal right to build cases against me and to bind me to every form of sickness and disease. I also repent for all self-inflicted word curses and covenants with demons that have existed in my ancestral bloodline. I am asking that every ancestral agreement with demonic powers and evil altars will now be revoked. I petition the courts of Heaven to silence their right to claim me and my bloodline, in Yeshua's name. Thank You, Lord, for revoking these demonically engineered covenants and evil altars in Yeshua's mighty name! Heavenly Father and Righteous Judge, it is my heartfelt desire to divorce myself from every form of sickness and disease that that is operating in my life. I petition the Ancient of Days to grant me a verdict of judicial emancipation from the oppressive power of sickness and disease. I receive Your favorable verdict by faith in Messiah's finished work and shed blood.

### 4. Petition the Courts of Heaven to Dismiss All of Satan's Charges

Heavenly Father and Righteous Judge, based upon Yeshua's finished work and my heartfelt repentance, I now move on the court of Heaven to dismiss all of satan's accusations and charges against me and my bloodline in Jesus's name. Righteous Judge, dismiss every one of satan's accusation connected to every form of sickness and disease that satan has weaponized against me. For it is written in Revelation 12:10 that the accuser of the brethren has been cast down. So, I petition You, heavenly Father and Righteous Judge, to cast down all of satan's accusations against me and dismiss all of satan's charges against me, in Yeshua's name, I pray.

## 5. Declare Your Authority in Christ

Heavenly Father and Righteous Judge, in Luke 10:19 (NKJV), Yeshua says, *"Behold, I give you the authority to trample on serpents and scorpions, and over all the power of the enemy, and nothing shall by any means hurt you."* Heavenly Father, as I prepare myself to pronounce powerful apostolic and prophetic decrees, I totally acknowledge my God-given authority in Christ to trample on serpents and scorpions that satan has weaponized against me and my destiny, in Yeshua's mighty name, I pray. The Bible also says in Proverbs 28:1 (NKJV), *"The wicked flee when no one pursues, but the righteous are bold as a lion."* Heavenly Father because of my God-given authority in Christ, I am as bold as lion. No messenger of satan, human or demonic, can intimidate me. I am like Mount Zion, which cannot be moved, in Yeshua's mighty name, I pray. I thank You, heavenly Father that in Mark 16:17-18, Yeshua gave me the authority to cast out devils and take up serpents and to bring God's healing power to those who are sick and oppressed. I therefore make the following decrees, completely assured of both my identity and authority in Christ Jesus!

## 6. Loudly Declare These Supernatural Decrees So You Can Have Your Breakthrough:

- Heavenly Father, I decree and declare that the power of every form of sickness and disease that satan has weaponized against me is completely broken. I decree that I am no longer a victim of these demonically engineered sicknesses and diseases, in Yeshua's name.

- I decree and declare that God is setting me free from every form of sickness and disease that causes physical and spiritual deafness in Yeshua's name.

- I decree and declare that the Holy Spirit is setting me free from any sickness or disease weaponized by any form of witchcraft or magic that is afflicting my body in any way, in Yeshua's name, I pray.

- I decree and declare that as I bring my sacrificial offering into the courts of Heaven, the power of every form of sickness and disease that satan is weaponizing against me is now destroyed, in Yeshua's name.

- I decree and declare that every form of sickness and disease that is behind any blood disorders is completely removed in Yeshua's mighty name!

- I decree and declare that God is setting me free from every disease, which has caused me to be crippled in Yeshua's name, I pray.

- I decree and declare that everything, which has been stolen from my life because of any form of sickness and disease that satan has weaponized against me is now be restored back to me, in Yeshua's name, I pray.

## 7. End with Thanksgiving

Heavenly Father and Righteous Judge, I thank You that the foundation of Your throne is righteousness and justice. Thank You for giving me justice against the demonic entities behind every form of sickness and disease. Heavenly Father, I thank You that because of the finished work of Yeshua on the Cross, You have translated me from the kingdom of darkness to Your glorious Kingdom of Light! Heavenly Father, since You have adopted me into Your divine family, I thank You that You always hear me, when I pray. I thank You that every apostolic and prophetic decree that I have made has been heard. Thank You, Lord, that everything I have just decreed is on its way to full manifestation in Yeshua's mighty name. Heavenly Father, until the manifestation, I will maintain an aggressive attitude of thanksgiving for the complete manifestation of what I have decreed today! In Yeshua's name I pray.

# Decrees for Silencing the Evil Moon

You shall not be afraid of the terror by night, nor of the arrow that flies by day, nor of the pestilence that walks in darkness, nor of the destruction that lays waste at noonday (**Psalm 91:5-6 NKJV**).

The sun shall not strike you by day, nor the moon by night (**Psalm 121:6 NKJV**).

## Prayer of Activation

### 1. Worship God

Heavenly Father, holy is Your name and greatly to be praised. You are the Father of Light and in You is no shadow of turning. I worship and adore You in Yeshua's name, for this purpose was I created, to give You pleasure through my love and adoration. May Your Kingdom manifest in my life as it is in Heaven. Plead my cause, O Lord, with those who strive with me; fight against any entity or person who is contending against me and what is written about me in Your book of destiny. Heavenly Father, it is written in Psalm 27:6 (NASB), *"And now my head will be lifted up above my enemies around me, and I will offer sacrifices in His tent with shouts of joy; I will sing, yes, I will sing praises to the Lord."* Heavenly Father, I thank You

that I will never be swallowed by the demonic powers because You are the Lifter of my head. Abba Father, I enjoin my worship to the heavenly chorus of worship of Your holy angels and the crowd of witnesses, in Yeshua's mighty name.

## 2. Enter the Courts of Heaven

Heavenly Father, Righteous Judge, I ask that the courts of Heaven be seated according to Daniel 7:9-10 (AMP) and that all books related to my life and destiny be opened. I ask this in Yeshua's mighty name. It is written: *"I kept looking until thrones were set up, and the Ancient of Days (God) took His seat; His garment was white as snow and the hair of His head like pure wool. His throne was flames of fire; its wheels were a burning fire. A river of fire was flowing and coming out from before Him; a thousand thousands were attending Him, and ten thousand times ten thousand were standing before Him; the court was seated, and the books were opened."* Heavenly Father, Righteous Judge, I am requesting the privilege of standing before the courtroom of the Ancient of Days according to what was revealed to the prophet Daniel, in Yeshua's name, I pray. Heavenly Father, I stand in Your royal courtroom because of the shed blood and finished work of Yeshua on the Cross. I have come to receive Your righteous judgment over my life against every demonic power generated from the moon that satan has been using against me. Heavenly Father, I call upon Your holy angels to be witnesses to my lawsuit and righteous prosecution of every demonic power generated from the moon that is working against me. I decree and declare that every demonic power generated from the moon covering my spirit, soul, and body is removed so I can achieve my God-given destiny here on earth, in Yeshua's name I pray.

## 3. Repent

Heavenly Father, Righteous Judge, it is written, *"If we confess our sins, He is faithful and just to forgive us our sins and to cleanse us from all unrighteousness"*

(1 John 1:9 NKJV). I therefore activate the law of repentance and present before this court my heartfelt repentance for my personal transgressions, and for the iniquities of my forefathers that opened the door for demonic powers generated from the moon to oppress my life and bloodline, in Yeshua's name I pray. Heavenly Father, I ask the blood of Yeshua wash away every iniquity of my forefathers that the enemy is using as a legal right to build cases against me and to bind me to every evil demonic power generated from the moon. I also repent for all self-inflicted word curses and covenants with demons that have existed in my ancestral bloodline. I am asking that every ancestral agreement with demonic powers and evil altars will now be revoked. I petition the courts of Heaven to silence their right to claim me and my bloodline, in Yeshua's name. Thank You, Lord, for revoking these demonically engineered covenants and evil altars in Yeshua's mighty name! Heavenly Father and Righteous Judge, it is my heartfelt desire to divorce myself from every demonic power generated from the moon that is operating in my life. I petition the Ancient of Days to grant me a verdict of judicial emancipation from the oppressive power of every demonic power generated from the moon. I receive Your favorable verdict by faith in Messiah's finished work and shed blood.

## 4. Petition the Courts of Heaven to Dismiss All of Satan's Charges

Heavenly Father and Righteous Judge, based upon Yeshua's finished work and my heartfelt repentance, I now move on the court of Heaven to dismiss all of satan's accusations and charges against me and my bloodline in Jesus's name. Righteous Judge, dismiss every one of satan's accusation connected to every demonic power generated from the moon that is oppressing my life. For it is written in Revelation 12:10 that the accuser of the brethren has been cast down. So, I petition You, heavenly Father and Righteous Judge, to cast down all of satan's accusations against me and dismiss all of satan's charges against me, in Yeshua's name, I pray.

## 5. Declare Your Authority in Christ

Heavenly Father and Righteous Judge, in Luke 10:19 (NKJV), Yeshua says, *"Behold, I give you the authority to trample on serpents and scorpions, and over all the power of the enemy, and nothing shall by any means hurt you."* Heavenly Father as I prepare myself to pronounce powerful apostolic and prophetic decrees, I totally acknowledge my God-given authority in Christ to trample on serpents and scorpions that satan has weaponized against me and my destiny, in Yeshua's mighty name, I pray. The Bible also says in Proverbs 28:1 (NKJV), *"The wicked flee when no one pursues, but the righteous are bold as a lion."* Heavenly Father because of my God-given authority in Christ, I am as bold as lion. No messenger of satan, human or demonic, can intimidate me. I am like Mount Zion, which cannot be moved, in Yeshua's mighty name, I pray. I thank You, heavenly Father, that in Mark 16:17-18, Yeshua gave me the authority to cast out devils and take up serpents and to bring God's healing power to those who are sick and oppressed. I therefore make the following decrees, completely assured of both my identity and authority in Christ Jesus!

## 6. Loudly Declare These Supernatural Decrees So You Can Have Your Breakthrough:

- Heavenly Father, I decree and declare that the power of every demonic aura generated from the moon of darkness is completely broken over my life. I decree that I am no longer a victim of any demonically engineered power of the moon, in Yeshua's name.

- I decree and declare that You are setting me free from every evil demonic power generated from the moon that causes physical and spiritual deafness in Yeshua's name.

- I decree and declare that the Holy Spirit is setting me free from any veil of witchcraft or magic connected to the moon that has caused any kind of spiritual blindness in my life, in Yeshua's name, I pray.

- I decree and declare that the Holy Spirit is setting me free from every demonic power generated from the moon that would cause me not to walk in the truthfulness of God's Word, in Yeshua's name, I pray.

- I decree and declare that as I bring my sacrificial offering into the courts of Heaven, every demonic power generated from the moon that satan placed over my finances is now destroyed, in Yeshua's name.

- I decree and declare that every demonic power generated from the moon covering my mind and stopping my spiritual and mental transformation according to Romans 12:1 is removed in Yeshua's mighty name!

- I decree and declare that God is setting me free from every demonic power generated from the moon, which has caused me to be spiritually crippled in Yeshua's name, I pray.

- I decree and declare that everything, which has been stolen from my life because of demonic powers generated from the moon, will now be restored back to me, in Yeshua's name, I pray.

## 7. End with Thanksgiving

Heavenly Father and Righteous Judge, I thank You that the foundation of Your throne is righteousness and justice. Thank You for giving me justice against the demonic entities behind evil powers generated from the moon. Heavenly Father, I thank You that because of the finished work of Yeshua on the Cross, You have translated me from the kingdom of darkness to Your glorious Kingdom of Light! Heavenly Father, since You have adopted me into Your divine family, I thank You that You always hear me, when I pray. I thank You that every apostolic and prophetic decree that I have made has been heard. Thank You, Lord, that everything I have just decreed is on its way to full manifestation in Yeshua's mighty name. Heavenly Father, until the manifestation, I will maintain an aggressive attitude of thanksgiving for the complete manifestation of what I have decreed today! In Yeshua's name I pray.

# Decrees for Silencing the Evil Power of the Sun

You shall not be afraid of the terror by night, nor of the arrow that flies by day, nor of the pestilence that walks in darkness, nor of the destruction that lays waste at noonday (**Psalm 91:5-6 NKJV**).

The sun shall not strike you by day, nor the moon by night (**Psalm 121:6 NKJV**).

## Prayer of Activation

### 1. Worship God

Heavenly Father, holy is Your name and greatly to be praised. You are the Father of Light and in You is no shadow of turning. I worship and adore You in Yeshua's name, for this purpose was I created, to give You pleasure through my love and adoration. May Your Kingdom manifest in my life as it is in Heaven. Plead my cause, O Lord, with those who strive with me; fight against any entity or person who is contending against me and what is written about me in Your book of destiny. Heavenly Father, it is written in Psalm 27:6 (NASB), *"And now my head will be lifted up above*

*my enemies around me, and I will offer sacrifices in His tent with shouts of joy; I will sing, yes, I will sing praises to the Lord."* Heavenly Father, I thank You that I will never be swallowed by the demonic powers because You are the Lifter of my head. Abba Father, I enjoin my worship to the heavenly chorus of worship of Your holy angels and the crowd of witnesses, in Yeshua's mighty name.

## 2. Enter the Courts of Heaven

Heavenly Father, Righteous Judge, I ask that the courts of Heaven be seated according to Daniel 7:9-10 (AMP) and that all books related to my life and destiny be opened. I ask this in Yeshua's mighty name. It is written: *"I kept looking until thrones were set up, and the Ancient of Days (God) took His seat; His garment was white as snow and the hair of His head like pure wool. His throne was flames of fire; its wheels were a burning fire. A river of fire was flowing and coming out from before Him; a thousand thousands were attending Him, and ten thousand times ten thousand were standing before Him; the court was seated, and the books were opened."* Heavenly Father, Righteous Judge, I am requesting the privilege of standing before the courtroom of the Ancient of Days according to what was revealed to the prophet Daniel, in Yeshua's name, I pray. Heavenly Father, I stand in Your royal courtroom because of the shed blood and finished work of Yeshua on the Cross. I have come to receive Your righteous judgment over my life against every demonic power generated from the sun that satan has been using against me. Heavenly Father, I call upon Your holy angels to be witnesses to my lawsuit and righteous prosecution of every demonic power generated from the sun that is working against me. I decree and declare that every demonic power generated from the sun covering my spirit, soul, and body will be removed so I can achieve my God-given destiny here on earth, in Yeshua's name I pray.

## 3. Repent

Heavenly Father, Righteous Judge, it is written, *"If we confess our sins, He is faithful and just to forgive us our sins and to cleanse us from all unrighteousness"* (1 John 1:9 NKJV). I therefore activate the law of repentance and present before this court my heartfelt repentance for my personal transgressions, and for the iniquities of my forefathers that opened the door for every demonically engineered power generated from the sun to oppress my life and bloodline, in Yeshua's name I pray. Heavenly Father, I ask that the blood of Yeshua wash away every iniquity of my forefathers that the enemy is using as a legal right to build cases against me and to bind me to every demonic power generated from the sun. I also repent for all self-inflicted word curses and covenants with demons that have existed in my ancestral bloodline. I am asking that every ancestral agreement with demonic powers and evil altars will now be revoked. I petition the courts of Heaven to silence their right to claim me and my bloodline, in Yeshua's name. Thank You, Lord, for revoking these demonically engineered covenants and evil altars in Yeshua's mighty name! Heavenly Father and Righteous Judge, it is my heartfelt desire to divorce myself from every demonic power generated from the sun that is operating in my life. I petition the Ancient of Days to grant me a verdict of judicial emancipation from the oppressive power of every demonically engineered power generated from the sun. I receive Your favorable verdict by faith in Messiah's finished work and shed blood.

## 4. Petition the Courts of Heaven to Dismiss All of Satan's Charges

Heavenly Father and Righteous Judge, based upon Yeshua's finished work and my heartfelt repentance, I now move on the court of Heaven to dismiss all of satan's accusations and charges against me and my bloodline in Jesus's name. Righteous Judge, dismiss every one of satan's accusation connected to every demonic power generated from the sun that is oppressing my life. For it is written in Revelation 12:10 that the accuser of the brethren has been cast down. So, I petition You, heavenly Father and Righteous Judge, to cast down all of satan's accusations against me and dismiss all of satan's charges against me, in Yeshua's name, I pray.

## 5. Declare Your Authority in Christ

Heavenly Father and Righteous Judge, in Luke 10:19 (NKJV), Yeshua says, *"Behold, I give you the authority to trample on serpents and scorpions, and over all the power of the enemy, and nothing shall by any means hurt you."* Heavenly Father as I prepare myself to pronounce powerful apostolic and prophetic decrees, I totally acknowledge my God-given authority in Christ to trample on serpents and scorpions that satan has weaponized against me and my destiny, in Yeshua's mighty name, I pray. The Bible also says in Proverbs 28:1 (NKJV), *"The wicked flee when no one pursues, but the righteous are bold as a lion."* Heavenly Father because of my God-given authority in Christ, I am as bold as lion. No messenger of satan, human or demonic, can intimidate me. I am like Mount Zion, which cannot be moved, in Yeshua's mighty name, I pray. I thank You, heavenly Father, that in Mark 16:17-18, Yeshua gave me the authority to cast out devils and take up serpents and to bring God's healing power to those who are sick and oppressed. I therefore make the following decrees, completely assured of both my identity and authority in Christ Jesus!

## 6. Loudly Declare These Supernatural Decrees So You Can Have Your Breakthrough:

- Heavenly Father, I decree and declare that every demonic power generated from the sun of darkness is completely broken over my life. I decree that I am no longer a victim of these demonic technologies of darkness, in Yeshua's name.

- I decree and declare that You are setting me free from every demonic power generated from the sun that causes physical and spiritual deafness in Yeshua's name.

- I decree and declare that the Holy Spirit is setting me free from any veil of witchcraft or magic connected to the sun that has caused any kind of spiritual blindness in my life, in Yeshua's name, I pray.

- I decree and declare that the Holy Spirit is setting me free from every demonic power generated from the sun that would cause me not to walk in the truthfulness of God's Word, in Yeshua's name, I pray.

- I decree and declare that as I bring my sacrificial offering into the courts of Heaven, every demonic power generated from the sun that satan placed over my finances is now destroyed, in Yeshua's name.

- I decree and declare that every demonic power generated from the sun covering my mind and stopping my spiritual and mental transformation according to Romans 12:1 is removed in Yeshua's mighty name!

- I decree and declare that God is setting me free from every demonic power generated from the sun, which has caused me to be spiritually crippled in Yeshua's name, I pray.

- I decree and declare that everything, which has been stolen from my life because of any demonically engineered power generated from the sun will now be restored back to me, in Yeshua's name, I pray.

## 7. End with Thanksgiving

Heavenly Father and Righteous Judge, I thank You that the foundation of Your throne is righteousness and justice. Thank You for giving me justice against the demonic entities behind the demonic power generated from the sun. Heavenly Father, I thank You that because of the finished work of Yeshua on the Cross, You have translated me from the kingdom of darkness to Your glorious Kingdom of Light! Heavenly Father, since You have adopted me into Your divine family, I thank You that You always hear me, when I pray. I thank You that every apostolic and prophetic decree that I have made has been heard. Thank You, Lord, that everything I have just decreed is on its way to full manifestation in Yeshua's mighty name. Heavenly Father, until the manifestation, I will maintain an aggressive attitude of thanksgiving for the complete manifestation of what I have decreed today! In Yeshua's name I pray.

# Decrees for Releasing Rivers of Prosperity

If they obey and serve Him, they shall spend their days in prosperity, and their years in pleasures (**Job 36:11 NKJV**).

## Prayer of Activation

### 1. Worship God

Heavenly Father, holy is Your name and greatly to be praised. You are the Father of Light and in You is no shadow of turning. I worship and adore You in Yeshua's name, for this purpose was I created, to give You pleasure through my love and adoration. May Your Kingdom manifest in my life as it is in Heaven. Plead my cause, O Lord, with those who strive with me; fight against any entity or person who is contending against me and what is written about me in Your book of destiny. Heavenly Father, it is written in Psalm 27:6 (NASB), *"And now my head will be lifted up above my enemies around me, and I will offer sacrifices in His tent with shouts of joy; I will sing, yes, I will sing praises to the Lord."* Heavenly Father, I thank You that I will never be swallowed by the demonic powers because You are the Lifter of my head. Abba Father, I enjoin my worship to the heavenly chorus of

worship of Your holy angels and the crowd of witnesses, in Yeshua's mighty name.

## 2. Enter the Courts of Heaven

Heavenly Father, Righteous Judge, I ask that the courts of Heaven be seated according to Daniel 7:9-10 (AMP) and that all books related to my life and destiny be opened. I ask this in Yeshua's mighty name. It is written: *"I kept looking until thrones were set up, and the Ancient of Days (God) took His seat; His garment was white as snow and the hair of His head like pure wool. His throne was flames of fire; its wheels were a burning fire. A river of fire was flowing and coming out from before Him; a thousand thousands were attending Him, and ten thousand times ten thousand were standing before Him; the court was seated, and the books were opened."* Heavenly Father, Righteous Judge, I am requesting the privilege of standing before the courtroom of the Ancient of Days according to what was revealed to the prophet Daniel, in Yeshua's name, I pray. Heavenly Father, I stand in Your royal courtroom because of the shed blood and finished work of Yeshua on the Cross. I have come to receive Your righteous judgment over my life against every evil scheme of satan that is working against my prosperity. Heavenly Father, I call upon Your holy angels to be witnesses to my lawsuit and righteous prosecution of every evil scheme of satan that is working against my prosperity. I decree and declare that every evil scheme of satan that is working against my prosperity will be removed so I can achieve my God-given destiny here on earth, in Yeshua's name I pray.

## 3. Repent

Heavenly Father, Righteous Judge, it is written, *"If we confess our sins, He is faithful and just to forgive us our sins and to cleanse us from all unrighteousness"* (1 John 1:9 NKJV). I therefore activate the law of repentance and present before this court my heartfelt repentance for my personal transgressions, and for the iniquities of my forefathers that opened the door for every evil scheme of satan to work against my prosperity in my life and bloodline, in Yeshua's name I pray. Heavenly Father, I ask that the blood of Yeshua wash away every iniquity of my forefathers that the enemy is using as a legal right to build cases against me and to bind me to every evil scheme of satan that is working against my prosperity. I also repent for all self-inflicted word curses and covenants with demons that have existed in my ancestral bloodline. I am asking that every ancestral agreement with demonic powers and evil altars will now be revoked. I petition the courts of Heaven to silence their right to claim me and my bloodline, in Yeshua's name. Thank You, Lord, for revoking these demonically engineered covenants and evil altars in Yeshua's mighty name! Heavenly Father and Righteous Judge, it is my heartfelt desire to divorce myself from every evil scheme of satan that is working against my prosperity. I petition the Ancient of Days to grant me a verdict of judicial emancipation from the oppressive power of every evil scheme of satan that is working against my prosperity. I receive Your favorable verdict by faith in Messiah's finished work and shed blood.

### 4. Petition the Courts of Heaven to Dismiss All of Satan's Charges

Heavenly Father and Righteous Judge, based upon Yeshua's finished work and my heartfelt repentance, I now move on the court of Heaven to dismiss all of satan's accusations and charges against me and my bloodline in Jesus's name. Righteous Judge, dismiss every one of satan's accusation connected to every evil scheme of satan that is working against my prosperity. For it is written in Revelation 12:10 that the accuser of the brethren has been cast down. So, I petition You, heavenly Father and Righteous Judge, to cast down all of satan's accusations against me and dismiss all of satan's charges against me, in Yeshua's name, I pray.

## 5. Declare Your Authority in Christ

Heavenly Father and Righteous Judge, in Luke 10:19 (NKJV), Yeshua says, *"Behold, I give you the authority to trample on serpents and scorpions, and over all the power of the enemy, and nothing shall by any means hurt you."* Heavenly Father, as I prepare myself to pronounce powerful apostolic and prophetic decrees, I totally acknowledge my God-given authority in Christ to trample on serpents and scorpions that satan has weaponized against me and my destiny, in Yeshua's mighty name, I pray. The Bible also says in Proverbs 28:1 (NKJV), *"The wicked flee when no one pursues, but the righteous are bold as a lion."* Heavenly Father, because of my God-given authority in Christ, I am as bold as lion. No messenger of satan, human or demonic, can intimidate me. I am like Mount Zion, which cannot be moved, in Yeshua's mighty name, I pray. I thank You, heavenly Father, that in Mark 16:17-18, Yeshua gave me the authority to cast out devils and take up serpents and to bring God's healing power to those who are sick and oppressed. I therefore make the following decrees, completely assured of both my identity and authority in Christ Jesus!

## 6. Loudly Declare These Supernatural Decrees So You Can Have Your Breakthrough:

- Heavenly Father I decree and declare that the power of every evil scheme of satan that is working against my prosperity is completely broken over my life. I decree that I am no longer a victim of these demonic assaults on my prosperity, in Yeshua's name.

- I decree and declare that You are setting me free from every evil scheme of satan that is working against my prosperity that causes physical and spiritual financial barrenness in Yeshua's name.

- I decree and declare that the Holy Spirit is setting me free from any spirit of witchcraft or magic that is working against my prosperity, in Yeshua's name, I pray.

- I decree and declare that the Holy Spirit is setting me free from every veil of deception that would cause me not to walk in the revelation on prosperity, in Yeshua's name, I pray.

- I decree and declare that as I bring my sacrificial offering into the courts of Heaven, the power of every evil stranglehold that satan placed over my finances is now destroyed, in Yeshua's name.

- I decree and declare that every evil veil of darkness covering my mind and stopping my spiritual and mental prosperity according to Romans 12:1 is removed in Yeshua's mighty name!

- I decree and declare that God is setting me free from every spirit of poverty and lack in Yeshua's name, I pray.

- I decree and declare that everything, which has been stolen from my life because of every evil scheme of satan working against my prosperity, will now be restored back to me, in Yeshua's name, I pray.

## 7. End with Thanksgiving

Heavenly Father and Righteous Judge, I thank You that the foundation of Your throne is righteousness and justice. Thank You for giving me justice against the demonic entities behind these evil schemes of satan, which are working against my prosperity. Heavenly Father, I thank You that because of the finished work of Yeshua on the Cross, You have translated me from the kingdom of darkness to Your glorious Kingdom of Light! Heavenly Father, since You have adopted me into Your divine family, I thank You that You always hear me, when I pray. I thank You that every apostolic and prophetic decree that I have made has been heard. Thank You, Lord, that everything I have just decreed is on its way to full manifestation in Yeshua's mighty name. Heavenly Father, until the manifestation, I will maintain an aggressive attitude of thanksgiving for the complete manifestation of what I have decreed today! In Yeshua's name I pray.

# Decrees for Opening Doors

I know your works. See, I have set before you an open door, and no one can shut it; for you have a little strength, have kept My word, and have not denied My name (**Revelation 3:8 NKJV**).

## Prayer of Activation

### 1. Worship God

Heavenly Father, holy is Your name and greatly to be praised. You are the Father of Light and in You is no shadow of turning. I worship and adore You in Yeshua's name, for this purpose was I created, to give You pleasure through my love and adoration. May Your Kingdom manifest in my life as it is in Heaven. Plead my cause, O Lord, with those who strive with me; fight against any entity or person who is contending against me and what is written about me in Your book of destiny. Heavenly Father, it is written in Psalm 27:6 (NASB), *"And now my head will be lifted up above my enemies around me, and I will offer sacrifices in His tent with shouts of joy; I will sing, yes, I will sing praises to the Lord."* Heavenly Father, I thank You that I will never be swallowed by the demonic powers because You are the Lifter of my head. Abba Father, I enjoin my worship to the heavenly chorus of worship of Your holy angels and the crowd of witnesses, in Yeshua's mighty name.

## 2. Enter the Courts of Heaven

Heavenly Father, Righteous Judge, I ask that the courts of Heaven be seated according to Daniel 7:9-10 (AMP) and that all books related to my life and destiny be opened. I ask this in Yeshua's mighty name. It is written: *"I kept looking until thrones were set up, and the Ancient of Days (God) took His seat; His garment was white as snow and the hair of His head like pure wool. His throne was flames of fire; its wheels were a burning fire. A river of fire was flowing and coming out from before Him; a thousand thousands were attending Him, and ten thousand times ten thousand were standing before Him; the court was seated, and the books were opened."* Heavenly Father, Righteous Judge, I am requesting the privilege of standing before the courtroom of the Ancient of Days according to what was revealed to the prophet Daniel, in Yeshua's name, I pray. Heavenly Father, I stand in Your royal courtroom because of the shed blood and finished work of Yeshua on the Cross. I have come to receive Your righteous judgment over my life against every demonic technology that satan has been using against me, to close "open doors" for my destiny. Heavenly Father, I call upon Your holy angels to be witnesses to my lawsuit and righteous prosecution of every demonic technology that satan has been using against me, to close "open doors" for my destiny. I decree and declare that every evil power covering my spirit, soul, and body will be removed so I can achieve my God-given destiny here on earth, in Yeshua's name I pray.

## 3. Repent

Heavenly Father, Righteous Judge, it is written, *"If we confess our sins, He is faithful and just to forgive us our sins and to cleanse us from all unrighteousness"* (1 John 1:9 NKJV). I therefore activate the law of repentance and present before this court my heartfelt repentance for my personal transgressions, and for the iniquities of my forefathers that opened the door for satan to oppress my life and bloodline, in Yeshua's name I pray. Heavenly Father, I ask that the blood of Yeshua wash away every iniquity of my forefathers that satan is using as a legal right against me, to close "open doors" for my destiny. I also repent for all self-inflicted word curses and covenants with demons that have existed in my ancestral bloodline. I am asking that every ancestral agreement with demonic powers and evil altars will now be revoked. I petition the courts of Heaven to silence their right to claim me and my bloodline, in Yeshua's name. Thank You, Lord, for revoking these demonically engineered covenants and evil altars in Yeshua's mighty name! Heavenly Father and Righteous Judge, it is my heartfelt desire to divorce myself from every spirit of darkness that is operating in my life. I petition the Ancient of Days to grant me a verdict of judicial emancipation from the oppressive power of every evil spirit fighting against open doors in my life and business. I receive Your favorable verdict by faith in Messiah's finished work and shed blood.

## 4. Petition the Courts of Heaven to Dismiss All of Satan's Charges

Heavenly Father and Righteous Judge, based upon Yeshua's finished work and my heartfelt repentance, I now move on the court of Heaven to dismiss all of satan's accusations and charges against me and my bloodline in Jesus's name. Righteous Judge, dismiss every one of satan's accusation connected to closing divinely orchestrated doors in my life. For it is written in Revelation 12:10 that the accuser of the brethren has been cast down. So, I petition You, heavenly Father and Righteous Judge, to cast down all of satan's accusations against me and dismiss all of satan's charges against me, in Yeshua's name, I pray.

## 5. Declare Your Authority in Christ

Heavenly Father and Righteous Judge, in Luke 10:19 (NKJV), Yeshua says, "*Behold, I give you the authority to trample on serpents and scorpions, and over all the power of the enemy, and nothing shall by any means hurt you.*" Heavenly Father as I prepare myself to pronounce powerful apostolic and prophetic decrees, I totally acknowledge my God-given authority in Christ to trample on serpents and scorpions that satan has weaponized against me and my destiny, in Yeshua's mighty name, I pray. The Bible also says in Proverbs 28:1 (NKJV), "*The wicked flee when no one pursues, but the righteous are bold as a lion.*" Heavenly Father because of my God-given authority in Christ, I am as bold as lion. No messenger of satan, human or demonic, can intimidate me. I am like Mount Zion, which cannot be moved, in Yeshua's mighty name, I pray. I thank You, heavenly Father, that in Mark 16:17-18, Yeshua gave me the authority to cast out devils and take up serpents and to bring God's healing power to those who are sick and oppressed. I therefore make the following decrees, completely assured of both my identity and authority in Christ Jesus!

## 6. Loudly Declare These Supernatural Decrees So You Can Have Your Breakthrough:

- Heavenly Father, I decree and declare that every evil power of darkness behind closed doors is completely broken over my life. I decree that I am no longer a victim of these demonic entities, in Yeshua's name.

- I decree and declare that You are setting me free from every evil spiritual power that causes delay because of closed doors in Yeshua's name.

- I decree and declare that the Holy Spirit is setting me free from any veil of witchcraft or magic that has led to the closing of divinely ordained doors in my life, in Yeshua's name, I pray.

- I decree and declare that the Holy Spirit is setting me free from every power of darkness that would cause me not to walk in these divinely ordained doors, in Yeshua's name, I pray.

- I decree and declare that as I bring my sacrificial offering into the courts of Heaven, the power of satan over my financial doors is now destroyed, in Yeshua's name.

- I decree and declare that God is setting me free from every evil scheme of satan, which has caused many divinely orchestrated doors in my life to close in Yeshua's name, I pray.

- I decree and declare that everything, which has been stolen from my life because of closed doors, will now be restored back to me, in Yeshua's name, I pray.

## 7. End with Thanksgiving

Heavenly Father and Righteous Judge, I thank You that the foundation of Your throne is righteousness and justice. Thank You for giving me justice against the demonic entities behind the demonic phenomenon of closed doors in my life. Heavenly Father, I thank You that because of the finished work of Yeshua on the Cross, You have translated me from the kingdom of darkness to Your glorious Kingdom of Light! Heavenly Father, since You have adopted me into Your divine family, I thank You that You always hear me, when I pray. I thank You that every apostolic and prophetic decree that I have made has been heard. Thank You, Lord, that everything I have just decreed is on its way to full manifestation in Yeshua's mighty name. Heavenly Father, until the manifestation, I will maintain an aggressive attitude of thanksgiving for the complete manifestation of what I have decreed today! In Yeshua's name I pray.

# Decrees for Silencing Water Spirits

In that day the Lord with His severe sword, great and strong, will punish Leviathan the fleeing serpent, Leviathan that twisted serpent; and He will slay the reptile that is in the sea (**Isaiah 27:1 NKJV**).

## Prayer of Activation

### 1. Worship God

Heavenly Father, holy is Your name and greatly to be praised. You are the Father of Light and in You is no shadow of turning. I worship and adore You in Yeshua's name, for this purpose was I created, to give You pleasure through my love and adoration. May Your Kingdom manifest in my life as it is in Heaven. Plead my cause, O Lord, with those who strive with me; fight against any entity or person who is contending against me and what is written about me in Your book of destiny. Heavenly Father, it is written in Psalm 27:6 (NASB), *"And now my head will be lifted up above my enemies around me, and I will offer sacrifices in His tent with shouts of joy; I will sing, yes, I will sing praises to the Lord."* Heavenly Father, I thank You that I will never be swallowed by the demonic powers because You are the Lifter of my head. Abba Father, I enjoin my worship to the heavenly chorus of

worship of Your holy angels and the crowd of witnesses, in Yeshua's mighty name.

## 2. Enter the Courts of Heaven

Heavenly Father, Righteous Judge, I ask that the courts of Heaven be seated according to Daniel 7:9-10 (AMP) and that all books related to my life and destiny be opened. I ask this in Yeshua's mighty name. It is written: *"I kept looking until thrones were set up, and the Ancient of Days (God) took His seat; His garment was white as snow and the hair of His head like pure wool. His throne was flames of fire; its wheels were a burning fire. A river of fire was flowing and coming out from before Him; a thousand thousands were attending Him, and ten thousand times ten thousand were standing before Him; the court was seated, and the books were opened."* Heavenly Father, Righteous Judge, I am requesting the privilege of standing before the courtroom of the Ancient of Days according to what was revealed to the prophet Daniel, in Yeshua's name, I pray. Heavenly Father, I stand in Your royal courtroom because of the shed blood and finished work of Yeshua on the Cross. I have come to receive Your righteous judgment over my life against every water spirit that satan has been using against me. Heavenly Father, I call upon Your holy angels to be witnesses to my lawsuit and righteous prosecution of every water spirit that is working against me. I decree and declare that every water spirit covering my spirit, soul, and body will be removed so I can achieve my God-given destiny here on earth, in Yeshua's name I pray.

## 3. Repent

Heavenly Father, Righteous Judge, it is written, *"If we confess our sins, He is faithful and just to forgive us our sins and to cleanse us from all unrighteousness"* (1 John 1:9 NKJV). I therefore activate the law of repentance and present before this court my heartfelt repentance for my personal transgressions, and for the iniquities of my forefathers that opened the door for every water spirit to oppress my life and bloodline, in Yeshua's name I pray. Heavenly Father, I ask that the blood of Yeshua wash away every iniquity of my fore-fathers that the enemy is using as a legal right to build cases against me and to bind me to the power of water spirits. I also repent for all self-inflicted word curses and covenants with demons that have existed in my ancestral bloodline. I am asking that every ancestral agreement with demonic powers and evil altars will now be revoked. I petition the courts of Heaven to silence their right to claim me and my bloodline, in Yeshua's name. Thank You, Lord, for revoking these demonically engineered covenants and evil altars in Yeshua's mighty name! Heavenly Father and Righteous Judge, it is my heartfelt desire to divorce myself from every water spirit that is operating in my life. I petition the Ancient of Days to grant me a verdict of judicial eman-cipation from the oppressive power of water spirits. I receive Your favorable verdict by faith in Messiah's finished work and shed blood.

## 4. Petition the Courts of Heaven to Dismiss All of Satan's Charges

Heavenly Father and Righteous Judge, based upon Yeshua's finished work and my heartfelt repentance, I now move on the Court of Heaven to dismiss all of satan's accusations and charges against me and my bloodline in Jesus's name. Righteous Judge, dismiss every one of satan's accusation connected to any water spirit that is oppressing my life. For it is written in Revelation 12:10 that the accuser of the brethren has been cast down. So, I petition You, heavenly Father and Righteous Judge, to cast down all of satan's accusations against me and dismiss all of satan's charges against me, in Yeshua's name, I pray.

## 5. Declare Your Authority in Christ

Heavenly Father and Righteous Judge, in Luke 10:19 (NKJV), Yeshua says, *"Behold, I give you the authority to trample on serpents and scorpions, and over all the power of the enemy, and nothing shall by any means hurt you."* Heavenly

Father, as I prepare myself to pronounce powerful apostolic and prophetic decrees, I totally acknowledge my God-given authority in Christ to trample on serpents and scorpions that satan has weaponized against me and my destiny, in Yeshua's mighty name, I pray. The Bible also says in Proverbs 28:1 (NKJV), *"The wicked flee when no one pursues, but the righteous are bold as a lion."* Heavenly Father because of my God-given authority in Christ, I am as bold as lion. No messenger of satan, human or demonic, can intimidate me. I am like Mount Zion, which cannot be moved, in Yeshua's mighty name, I pray. I thank You, heavenly Father, that in Mark 16:17-18, Yeshua gave me the authority to cast out devils and take up serpents and to bring God's healing power to those who are sick and oppressed. I therefore make the following decrees, completely assured of both my identity and authority in Christ Jesus!

### 6. Loudly Declare These Supernatural Decrees So You Can Have Your Breakthrough:

- Heavenly Father, I decree and declare that the power of every water spirit is completely broken over my life. I decree that I am no longer a victim of these water spirits, in Yeshua's name.

- I decree and declare that You are setting me free from every water spirit that causes physical and spiritual deafness in Yeshua's name.

- I decree and declare that the Holy Spirit is setting me free from any veil of witchcraft or magic connected to water spirits that has caused any kind of spiritual blindness in my life, in Yeshua's name, I pray.

- I decree and declare that the Holy Spirit is setting me free from every water spirit that would cause me not to walk in the truthfulness of God's Word, in Yeshua's name, I pray.

- I decree and declare that as I bring my sacrificial offering into the courts of Heaven, the power of every water spirit that satan has placed over my finances is now destroyed, in Yeshua's name.

- I decree and declare that every water spirit covering my mind and stopping my spiritual and mental transformation according to Romans 12:1 is removed in Yeshua's mighty name!

- I decree and declare that God is setting me free from every water spirit, which has caused me to be spiritually crippled in Yeshua's name, I pray.

- I decree and declare that everything, which has been stolen from my life because of water spirits, will now be restored back to me, in Yeshua's name, I pray.

## 7. End with Thanksgiving

Heavenly Father and Righteous Judge, I thank You that the foundation of Your throne is righteousness and justice. Thank You for giving me justice against the demonic entities behind these water spirits. Heavenly Father, I thank You that because of the finished work of Yeshua on the Cross, You have translated me from the kingdom of darkness to Your glorious Kingdom of Light! Heavenly Father, since You have adopted me into Your divine family, I thank You that You always hear me, when I pray. I thank You that every apostolic and prophetic decree that I have made has been heard. Thank You, Lord, that everything I have just decreed is on its way to full manifestation in Yeshua's mighty name. Heavenly Father, until the manifestation, I will maintain an aggressive attitude of thanksgiving for the complete manifestation of what I have decreed today! In Yeshua's name I pray.

# Decrees for Overthrowing the Spirit of Fear

There is no fear in love; but perfect love casts out fear, because fear involves torment. But he who fears has not been made perfect in love (**1 John 4:18 NKJV**).

For God has not given us a spirit of fear, but of power and of love and of a sound mind (**2 Timothy 1:7 NKJV**).

## Prayer of Activation

### 1. Worship God

Heavenly Father, holy is Your name and greatly to be praised. You are the Father of Light and in You is no shadow of turning. I worship and adore You in Yeshua's name, for this purpose was I created, to give You pleasure through my love and adoration. May Your Kingdom manifest in my life as it is in Heaven. Plead my cause, O Lord, with those who strive with me; fight against any entity or person who is contending against me and what is written about me in Your book of destiny. Heavenly Father, it is written in Psalm 27:6 (NASB), *"And now my head will be lifted up above*

*my enemies around me, and I will offer sacrifices in His tent with shouts of joy; I will sing, yes, I will sing praises to the Lord."* Heavenly Father, I thank You that I will never be swallowed by the demonic powers because You are the Lifter of my head. Abba Father, I enjoin my worship to the heavenly chorus of worship of Your holy angels and the crowd of witnesses, in Yeshua's mighty name.

## 2. Enter the Courts of Heaven

Heavenly Father, Righteous Judge, I ask that the courts of Heaven be seated according to Daniel 7:9-10 (AMP) and that all books related to my life and destiny be opened. I ask this in Yeshua's mighty name. It is written: *"I kept looking until thrones were set up, and the Ancient of Days (God) took His seat; His garment was white as snow and the hair of His head like pure wool. His throne was flames of fire; its wheels were a burning fire. A river of fire was flowing and coming out from before Him; a thousand thousands were attending Him, and ten thousand times ten thousand were standing before Him; the court was seated, and the books were opened."* Heavenly Father, Righteous Judge, I am requesting the privilege of standing before the courtroom of the Ancient of Days according to what was revealed to the prophet Daniel, in Yeshua's name, I pray. Heavenly Father, I stand in Your royal courtroom because of the shed blood and finished work of Yeshua on the Cross. I have come to receive Your righteous judgment over my life against every spirit of fear that satan has been using against me. Heavenly Father, I call upon Your holy angels to be witnesses to my lawsuit and righteous prosecution of every spirit of fear that is working against me. I decree and declare that every spirit of fear covering my spirit, soul, and body will be removed so I can achieve my God-given destiny here on earth, in Yeshua's name I pray.

## 3. Repent

Heavenly Father, Righteous Judge, it is written, *"If we confess our sins, He is faithful and just to forgive us our sins and to cleanse us from all unrighteousness"* (1 John 1:9 NKJV). I therefore activate the law of repentance and present before this court my heartfelt repentance for my personal transgressions, and for the iniquities of my forefathers that opened the door for the spirit of fear to oppress my life and bloodline, in Yeshua's name I pray. Heavenly Father, I ask that the blood of Yeshua wash away every iniquity of my forefathers that the enemy is using as a legal right to build cases against me and to bind me to the spirit of fear. I also repent for all self-inflicted word curses and covenants with demons that have existed in my ancestral bloodline. I am asking that every ancestral agreement with demonic powers and evil altars will now be revoked. I petition the courts of Heaven to silence their right to claim me and my bloodline, in Yeshua's name. Thank You, Lord, for revoking these demonically engineered covenants and evil altars in Yeshua's mighty name! Heavenly Father and Righteous Judge, it is my heartfelt desire to divorce myself from every spirit of fear that is operating in my life. I petition the Ancient of Days to grant me a verdict of judicial emancipation from the oppressive power of every spirit of fear. I receive Your favorable verdict by faith in Messiah's finished work and shed blood.

## 4. Petition the Courts of Heaven to Dismiss All of Satan's Charges

Heavenly Father and Righteous Judge, based upon Yeshua's finished work and my heartfelt repentance, I now move on the court of Heaven to dismiss all of satan's accusations and charges against me and my bloodline in Jesus's name. Righteous Judge, dismiss every one of satan's accusation connected to every spirit of fear that is oppressing my life. For it is written in Revelation 12:10 that the accuser of the brethren has been cast down. So, I petition You Heavenly Father and Righteous Judge to cast down all of satan's accusations against me and dismiss all of satan's charges against me, in Yeshua's name, I pray.

## 5. Declare Your Authority in Christ

Heavenly Father and Righteous Judge, in Luke 10:19 (NKJV), Yeshua says, *"Behold, I give you the authority to trample on serpents and scorpions, and over all the power of the enemy, and nothing shall by any means hurt you."* Heavenly Father, as I prepare myself to pronounce powerful apostolic and prophetic decrees, I totally acknowledge my God-given authority in Christ to trample on serpents and scorpions that satan has weaponized against me and my destiny, in Yeshua's mighty name, I pray. The Bible also says in Proverbs 28:1 (NKJV), *"The wicked flee when no one pursues, but the righteous are bold as a lion."* Heavenly Father because of my God-given authority in Christ, I am as bold as lion. No messenger of satan, human or demonic, can intimidate me. I am like Mount Zion, which cannot be moved, in Yeshua's mighty name, I pray. I thank You, heavenly Father, that in Mark 16:17-18, Yeshua gave me the authority to cast out devils and take up serpents and to bring God's healing power to those who are sick and oppressed. I therefore make the following decrees, completely assured of both my identity and authority in Christ Jesus!

## 6. Loudly Declare These Supernatural Decrees So You Can Have Your Breakthrough:

- Heavenly Father, I decree and declare that the power of every spirit of fear is completely broken over my life. I decree that I am no longer a victim of the spirit of fear, in Yeshua's name.

- I decree and declare that You are setting me free from every spirit of fear that causes physical and spiritual deafness in Yeshua's name.

- I decree and declare that the Holy Spirit is setting me free from any veil of witchcraft or magic connected to the spirit of fear that has caused any kind of spiritual blindness in my life, in Yeshua's name, I pray.

- I decree and declare that the Holy Spirit is setting me free from every spirit of fear that would cause me not to walk in the truthfulness of God's Word, in Yeshua's name, I pray.

- I decree and declare that as I bring my sacrificial offering into the courts of Heaven, the power of every spirit of fear that satan placed over my finances is now destroyed, in Yeshua's name.

- I decree and declare that every spirit of fear covering my mind and stopping my spiritual and mental transformation according to Romans 12:1 is removed in Yeshua's mighty name!

- I decree and declare that God is setting me free from every spirit of fear, which has caused me to be spiritually crippled in Yeshua's name, I pray.

- I decree and declare that everything, which has been stolen from my life because of the spirit of fear, will now be restored back to me, in Yeshua's name, I pray.

## 7. End with Thanksgiving

Heavenly Father and Righteous Judge, I thank You that the foundation of Your throne is righteousness and justice. Thank You for giving me justice against the demonic entities behind the spirit of fear. Heavenly Father, I thank You that because of the finished work of Yeshua on the Cross, You have translated me from the kingdom of darkness to Your glorious Kingdom of Light! Heavenly Father, since You have adopted me into Your divine family, I thank You that You always hear me, when I pray. I thank You that every apostolic and prophetic decree that I have made has been heard. Thank You, Lord, that everything I have just decreed is on its way to full manifestation in Yeshua's mighty name. Heavenly Father, until the manifestation, I will maintain an aggressive attitude of thanksgiving for the complete manifestation of what I have decreed today! In Yeshua's name I pray.

# Decrees for Opening Up the Courts of Heaven

I watched till thrones were put in place, and the Ancient of Days was seated; His garment was white as snow, and the hair of His head was like pure wool. His throne was a fiery flame, its wheels a burning fire; a fiery stream issued and came forth from before Him. A thousand thousands ministered to Him; ten thousand times ten thousand stood before Him. The court was seated, and the books were opened (**Daniel 7:9-10 NKJV**).

## Prayer of Activation

### 1. Worship God

Heavenly Father, holy is Your name and greatly to be praised. You are the Father of Light and in You is no shadow of turning. I worship and adore You in Yeshua's name, for this purpose was I created, to give You pleasure through my love and adoration. May Your Kingdom manifest in my life as it is in Heaven. Plead my cause, O Lord, with those who strive with me; fight against any entity or person who is contending against me and what is written about me in Your book of destiny. Heavenly Father,

it is written in Psalm 27:6 (NASB), *"And now my head will be lifted up above my enemies around me, and I will offer sacrifices in His tent with shouts of joy; I will sing, yes, I will sing praises to the Lord."* Heavenly Father, I thank You that I will never be swallowed by the demonic powers because You are the Lifter of my head. Abba Father, I enjoin my worship to the heavenly chorus of worship of Your holy angels and the crowd of witnesses, in Yeshua's mighty name.

## 2. Enter the Courts of Heaven

Heavenly Father, Righteous Judge, I ask that the courts of Heaven be seated according to Daniel 7:9-10 (AMP) and that all books related to my life and destiny be opened. I ask this in Yeshua's mighty name. It is written: *"I kept looking until thrones were set up, and the Ancient of Days (God) took His seat; His garment was white as snow and the hair of His head like pure wool. His throne was flames of fire; its wheels were a burning fire. A river of fire was flowing and coming out from before Him; a thousand thousands were attending Him, and ten thousand times ten thousand were standing before Him; the court was seated, and the books were opened."* Heavenly Father, Righteous Judge, I am requesting the privilege of standing before the courtroom of the Ancient of Days according to what was revealed to the prophet Daniel, in Yeshua's name, I pray. Heavenly Father, I stand in Your royal courtroom because of the shed blood and finished work of Yeshua on the Cross. I have come to receive Your righteous judgment over my life against every accusation that satan has been using against me in the courts of Heaven. Heavenly Father, I call upon Your holy angels to be witnesses to my petition to open up the courts of Heaven over the affairs of my life, in Yeshua's name I pray.

## 3. Repent

Heavenly Father, Righteous Judge, it is written, *"If we confess our sins, He is faithful and just to forgive us our sins and to cleanse us from all unrighteousness"*

(1 John 1:9 NKJV). I therefore activate the law of repentance and present before this court my heartfelt repentance for my personal transgressions, and for the iniquities of my forefathers that opened the door for satan to accuse my life and bloodline, in Yeshua's name I pray. Heavenly Father, I ask that the blood of Yeshua wash away every iniquity of my forefathers that the enemy is using as a legal right to build cases against me in the courts of Heaven. I also repent for all self-inflicted word curses and covenants with demons that have existed in my ancestral bloodline. I am asking that every ancestral agreement with demonic powers and evil altars will now be revoked. I petition the courts of Heaven to silence their right to claim me and my bloodline, in Yeshua's name. Thank You, Lord, for revoking these demonically engineered covenants and evil altars in Yeshua's mighty name! I petition the Ancient of Days to grant me a verdict of judicial emancipation from any oppressive power of darkness operating against me in the courts of Heaven. I receive Your favorable verdict by faith in Messiah's finished work and shed blood.

### 4. Petition the Courts of Heaven to Dismiss All of Satan's Charges

Heavenly Father and Righteous Judge, based upon Yeshua's finished work and my heartfelt repentance, I now move on the court of Heaven to dismiss all of satan's accusations and charges against me and my bloodline in Jesus's name. Righteous Judge, dismiss every one of satan's accusation and charges standing against me in the courts of Heaven. For it is written in Revelation 12:10 that the accuser of the brethren has been cast down. So, I petition You, heavenly Father and Righteous Judge, to cast down all of satan's accusations against me and dismiss all of satan's charges against me, in Yeshua's name, I pray.

## 5. Declare Your Authority in Christ

Heavenly Father and Righteous Judge, in Luke 10:19 (NKJV), Yeshua says, *"Behold, I give you the authority to trample on serpents and scorpions, and over all the power of the enemy, and nothing shall by any means hurt you."* Heavenly Father, as I prepare myself to pronounce powerful apostolic and prophetic decrees, I totally acknowledge my God-given authority in Christ to trample on serpents and scorpions that satan has weaponized against me and my destiny, in Yeshua's mighty name, I pray. The Bible also says in Proverbs 28:1 (NKJV), *"The wicked flee when no one pursues, but the righteous are bold as a lion."* Heavenly Father, because of my God-given authority in Christ, I am as bold as lion. No messenger of satan, human or demonic, can intimidate me. I am like Mount Zion, which cannot be moved, in Yeshua's mighty name, I pray. I thank You, heavenly Father, that in Mark 16:17-18, Yeshua gave me the authority to cast out devils and take up serpents and to bring God's healing power to those who are sick and oppressed. I therefore make the following decrees, completely assured of both my identity and authority in Christ Jesus!

## 6. Loudly Declare These Supernatural Decrees So You Can Have Your Breakthrough:

- Heavenly Father, I decree and declare that the courts of Heaven are open for me to prevail against every power of darkness. I decree that I am no longer a victim of satan's accusations and charges, in Yeshua's name.

- I decree and declare that You are setting me free from every verdict that satan has ever won against me in the courts of Heaven, in Yeshua's name.

- I decree and declare that the Holy Spirit is setting me free from any veil of witchcraft or magic by moving the courts of Heaven in my favor, in Yeshua's name, I pray.

- I decree and declare that the Holy Spirit is opening the courts of Heaven to silence every evil power against me, in Yeshua's name, I pray.

- I decree and declare that as I bring my sacrificial offering into the courts of Heaven, the power of every evil spirit that satan placed over my finances is now destroyed, in Yeshua's name.

- I decree and declare that the courts of Heaven are open on my behalf and my books of destiny are also open in Yeshua's mighty name!

- I decree and declare that God is issuing divine restraining orders against the enemy on my behalf, in Yeshua's name, I pray.

## 7. End with Thanksgiving

Heavenly Father and Righteous Judge, I thank You that the foundation of Your throne is righteousness and justice. Thank You for opening the courts of Heaven on my behalf. Heavenly Father, I thank You that because of the finished work of Yeshua on the Cross, You have translated me from the kingdom of darkness to Your glorious Kingdom of Light! Heavenly Father, since You have adopted me into Your divine family, I thank You that You always hear me, when I pray. I thank You that every apostolic and prophetic decree that I have made has been heard. Thank You, Lord, that everything I have just decreed is on its way to full manifestation in Yeshua's mighty name. Heavenly Father, until the manifestation, I will maintain an aggressive attitude of thanksgiving for the complete manifestation of what I have decreed today! In Yeshua's name I pray.

# Decrees for Selling or Buying Real Estate

"My lord, listen to me; the land is worth four hundred shekels of silver. What is that between you and me? So bury your dead." And Abraham listened to Ephron; and Abraham weighed out the silver for Ephron which he had named in the hearing of the sons of Heth, four hundred shekels of silver, currency of the merchants (**Genesis 23:15-16 NKJV**).

## Prayer of Activation

### 1. Worship God

Heavenly Father, holy is Your name and greatly to be praised. You are the Father of Light and in You is no shadow of turning. I worship and adore You in Yeshua's name, for this purpose was I created, to give You pleasure through my love and adoration. May Your Kingdom manifest in my life as it is in Heaven. Plead my cause, O Lord, with those who strive with me; fight against any entity or person who is contending against me and what is written about me in Your book of destiny. Heavenly Father, it is written in Psalm 27:6 (NASB), *"And now my head will be lifted up above*

*my enemies around me, and I will offer sacrifices in His tent with shouts of joy; I will sing, yes, I will sing praises to the Lord."* Heavenly Father, I thank You that I will never be swallowed by the demonic powers because You are the Lifter of my head. Abba Father, I enjoin my worship to the heavenly chorus of worship of Your holy angels and the crowd of witnesses, in Yeshua's mighty name.

## 2. Enter the Courts of Heaven

Heavenly Father, Righteous Judge, I ask that the courts of Heaven be seated according to Daniel 7:9-10 (AMP) and that all books related to my life and destiny be opened. I ask this in Yeshua's mighty name. It is written: *"I kept looking until thrones were set up, and the Ancient of Days (God) took His seat; His garment was white as snow and the hair of His head like pure wool. His throne was flames of fire; its wheels were a burning fire. A river of fire was flowing and coming out from before Him; a thousand thousands were attending Him, and ten thousand times ten thousand were standing before Him; the court was seated, and the books were opened."* Heavenly Father, Righteous Judge, I am requesting the privilege of standing before the courtroom of the Ancient of Days according to what was revealed to the prophet Daniel, in Yeshua's name, I pray. Heavenly Father, I stand in Your royal courtroom because of the shed blood and finished work of Yeshua on the Cross. I have come to receive Your righteous judgment over my life against every evil veil or power of satan that is stopping me from buying or selling real estate. Heavenly Father, I call upon Your holy angels to be witnesses to my lawsuit and righteous prosecution of every evil veil or power of satan that is stopping me from buying or selling real estate. I decree and declare that every evil veil or power of satan covering my piece of real estate is removed, in Yeshua's name I pray.

## 3. Repent

Heavenly Father, Righteous Judge, it is written, *"If we confess our sins, He is faithful and just to forgive us our sins and to cleanse us from all unrighteousness"* (1 John 1:9 NKJV). I therefore activate the law of repentance and present before this court my heartfelt repentance for my personal transgressions, and for the iniquities of my forefathers that opened the door for every evil veil or power of satan that is stopping me from buying or selling real estate, in Yeshua's name I pray. Heavenly Father, I ask that the blood of Yeshua wash away every iniquity of my forefathers that the enemy is using as a legal right to build cases against me and to stop me from buying or selling real estate. I also repent for all self-inflicted word curses and covenants with demons that have existed in my ancestral bloodline. I am asking that every ancestral agreement with demonic powers and evil altars will now be revoked. I petition the courts of Heaven to silence their right to claim me and my bloodline, in Yeshua's name. Thank You, Lord, for revoking these demonically engineered covenants and evil altars in Yeshua's mighty name! Heavenly Father and Righteous Judge, it is my heartfelt desire to divorce myself from every evil of darkness that is stopping me from buying or selling real estate. I petition the Ancient of Days to grant me a verdict of judicial emancipation from the oppressive power of every evil veil or power of darkness that is stopping me from buying or selling real estate. I receive Your favorable verdict by faith in Messiah's finished work and shed blood.

## 4. Petition the Courts of Heaven to Dismiss All of Satan's Charges

Heavenly Father and Righteous Judge, based upon Yeshua's finished work and my heartfelt repentance, I now move on the Court of Heaven to dismiss all of satan's accusations and charges against me and my bloodline in Jesus's name. Righteous Judge, dismiss every one of satan's accusation connected to every evil veil or power of darkness that is stopping me from buying or selling real estate. For it is written in Revelation 12:10 that the accuser of the brethren has been cast down. So, I petition You, heavenly Father and Righteous Judge, to cast down all of satan's accusations against me and dismiss all of satan's charges against me, in Yeshua's name, I pray.

## 5. Declare Your Authority in Christ

Heavenly Father and Righteous Judge, in Luke 10:19 (NKJV), Yeshua says, *"Behold, I give you the authority to trample on serpents and scorpions, and over all the power of the enemy, and nothing shall by any means hurt you."* Heavenly Father, as I prepare myself to pronounce powerful apostolic and prophetic decrees, I totally acknowledge my God-given authority in Christ to trample on serpents and scorpions that satan has weaponized against me and my destiny, in Yeshua's mighty name, I pray. The Bible also says in Proverbs 28:1 (NKJV), *"The wicked flee when no one pursues, but the righteous are bold as a lion."* Heavenly Father, because of my God-given authority in Christ, I am as bold as lion. No messenger of satan, human or demonic, can intimidate me. I am like Mount Zion, which cannot be moved, in Yeshua's mighty name, I pray. I thank You, heavenly Father, that in Mark 16:17-18, Yeshua gave me the authority to cast out devils and take up serpents and to bring God's healing power to those who are sick and oppressed. I therefore make the following decrees, completely assured of both my identity and authority in Christ Jesus!

## 6. Loudly Declare These Supernatural Decrees So You Can Have Your Breakthrough:

- Heavenly Father, I decree and declare that the power of every evil veil or power of darkness that is stopping me from buying or selling real estate is completely broken over my life. I decree that I am no longer a victim of these demonic technologies, in Yeshua's name.

- I decree and declare that You are setting me free from every evil veil or power of darkness that has robbed me of real estate in Yeshua's name.

- I decree and declare that the Holy Spirit is setting me free from any veil of witchcraft or magic that is stopping me from buying or selling real estate, in Yeshua's name, I pray.

- I decree and declare that the Holy Spirit is setting me free from every evil veil or power of darkness that is driving away customers from my real estate business, in Yeshua's name, I pray.

- I decree and declare that as I bring my sacrificial offering into the courts of Heaven, the power of every evil veil that satan placed over finances I am supposed to generate from real estate is now destroyed, in Yeshua's name.

- I decree and declare that every evil veil of darkness covering my real estate from being sold is removed in Yeshua's mighty name!

- I decree and declare that everything, every real estate which has been stolen from me or my bloodline, will now be restored back to me, in Yeshua's name, I pray.

## 7. End with Thanksgiving

Heavenly Father and Righteous Judge, I thank You that the foundation of Your throne is righteousness and justice. Thank You for giving me justice against the demonic entities behind my failure to buy or sell real estate. Heavenly Father, I thank You that because of the finished work of Yeshua on the Cross, You have translated me from the kingdom of darkness to Your glorious Kingdom of Light! Heavenly Father, since You have adopted me into Your divine family, I thank You that You always hear me, when I pray. I thank You that every apostolic and prophetic decree that I have made has been heard. Thank You, Lord, that everything I have just decreed is on its way to full manifestation in Yeshua's mighty name. Heavenly Father, until the manifestation, I will maintain an aggressive attitude of thanksgiving for the complete manifestation of what I have decreed today! In Yeshua's name I pray.

# Decrees for Releasing the Fire of God

When Solomon had finished praying, fire came down from heaven and consumed the burnt offering and the sacrifices; and the glory of the Lord filled the temple. And the priests could not enter the house of the Lord, because the glory of the Lord had filled the Lord's house. When all the children of Israel saw how the fire came down, and the glory of the Lord on the temple, they bowed their faces to the ground on the pavement, and worshiped and praised the Lord, saying: "For He is good, for His mercy endures forever" (**2 Chronicles 7:1-3 NKJV**).

## Prayer of Activation

### 1. Worship God

Heavenly Father, holy is Your name and greatly to be praised. You are the Father of Light and in You is no shadow of turning. I worship and adore You in Yeshua's name, for this purpose was I created, to give You pleasure through my love and adoration. May Your Kingdom manifest in my life as it is in Heaven. Plead my cause, O Lord, with those who strive with me; fight against any entity or person who is contending against me and what is written about me in Your book of destiny. Heavenly Father,

it is written in Psalm 27:6 (NASB), *"And now my head will be lifted up above my enemies around me, and I will offer sacrifices in His tent with shouts of joy; I will sing, yes, I will sing praises to the Lord."* Heavenly Father, I thank You that I will never be swallowed by the demonic powers because You are the Lifter of my head. Abba Father, I enjoin my worship to the heavenly chorus of worship of Your holy angels and the crowd of witnesses, in Yeshua's mighty name.

## 2. Enter the Courts of Heaven

Heavenly Father, Righteous Judge, I ask that the courts of Heaven be seated according to Daniel 7:9-10 (AMP) and that all books related to my life and destiny be opened. I ask this in Yeshua's mighty name. It is written: *"I kept looking until thrones were set up, and the Ancient of Days (God) took His seat; His garment was white as snow and the hair of His head like pure wool. His throne was flames of fire; its wheels were a burning fire. A river of fire was flowing and coming out from before Him; a thousand thousands were attending Him, and ten thousand times ten thousand were standing before Him; the court was seated, and the books were opened."* Heavenly Father, Righteous Judge, I am requesting the privilege of standing before the courtroom of the Ancient of Days according to what was revealed to the prophet Daniel, in Yeshua's name, I pray. Heavenly Father, I stand in Your royal courtroom because of the shed blood and finished work of Yeshua on the Cross. I have come to receive Your righteous judgment over my life against every scheme of satan that is keeping me from walking in the fire of God. Heavenly Father, I call upon Your holy angels to be witnesses to my lawsuit and righteous prosecution of every scheme of satan that is keeping me from walking in the fire of God. I decree and declare that every scheme of satan covering my spirit, soul, and body will be removed so I can walk in the fire of God, in Yeshua's name I pray.

## 3. Repent

Heavenly Father, Righteous Judge, it is written, *"If we confess our sins, He is faithful and just to forgive us our sins and to cleanse us from all unrighteousness"* (1 John 1:9 NKJV). I therefore activate the law of repentance and present before this court my heartfelt repentance for my personal transgressions, and for the iniquities of my forefathers that opened the door for the powers of darkness to oppress my life and bloodline, in Yeshua's name I pray. Heavenly Father, I ask that the blood of Yeshua wash away every iniquity of my forefathers that the enemy is using as a legal right to build cases against me and to bind me to every scheme of satan that is keeping me from walking in the fire of God. I also repent for all self-inflicted word curses and covenants with demons that have existed in my ancestral bloodline. I am asking that every ancestral agreement with demonic powers and evil altars will now be revoked. I petition the courts of Heaven to silence their right to claim me and my bloodline, in Yeshua's name. Thank You, Lord, for revoking these demonically engineered covenants and evil altars in Yeshua's mighty name! Heavenly Father and Righteous Judge, it is my heartfelt desire to divorce myself from every scheme of satan that is keeping me from walking in the fire of God. I petition the Ancient of Days to grant me a verdict of judicial emancipation from the oppressive power of every scheme of satan that is keeping me from walking in the fire of God. I receive Your favorable verdict by faith in Messiah's finished work and shed blood.

## 4. Petition the Courts of Heaven to Dismiss All of Satan's Charges

Heavenly Father and Righteous Judge, based upon Yeshua's finished work and my heartfelt repentance, I now move on the Court of Heaven to dismiss all of satan's accusations and charges against me and my bloodline in Jesus's name. Righteous Judge, dismiss every one of satan's accusation connected to every scheme of satan that is keeping me from walking in the fire of God. For it is written in Revelation 12:10 that the accuser of the brethren has been cast down. So, I petition You, heavenly Father and Righteous Judge, to cast down all of satan's accusations against me and dismiss all of satan's charges against me, in Yeshua's name, I pray.

## 5. Declare Your Authority in Christ

Heavenly Father and Righteous Judge, in Luke 10:19 (NKJV), Yeshua says, *"Behold, I give you the authority to trample on serpents and scorpions, and over all the power of the enemy, and nothing shall by any means hurt you."* Heavenly Father as I prepare myself to pronounce powerful apostolic and prophetic decrees, I totally acknowledge my God-given authority in Christ to trample on serpents and scorpions that satan has weaponized against me and my destiny, in Yeshua's mighty name, I pray. The Bible also says in Proverbs 28:1 (NKJV), *"The wicked flee when no one pursues, but the righteous are bold as a lion."* Heavenly Father because of my God-given authority in Christ, I am as bold as lion. No messenger of satan, human or demonic, can intimidate me. I am like Mount Zion, which cannot be moved, in Yeshua's mighty name, I pray. I thank You, heavenly Father, that in Mark 16:17-18, Yeshua gave me the authority to cast out devils and take up serpents and to bring God's healing power to those who are sick and oppressed. I therefore make the following decrees, completely assured of both my identity and authority in Christ Jesus!

## 6. Loudly Declare These Supernatural Decrees So You Can Have Your Breakthrough:

- Heavenly Father, I decree and declare that the power of every scheme of satan that is keeping me from walking in the fire of God is completely broken over my life. I decree that I am no longer a victim of these demonic technologies, in Yeshua's name.

- I decree and declare that You are setting me free from every form of spiritual dryness in Yeshua's name.

- I decree and declare that the Holy Spirit is setting me free from any form of witchcraft or magic that is keeping me from walking in the fire of God, in Yeshua's name, I pray.

- I decree and declare that the Holy Spirit is setting me free from every veil of deception that is keeping me from walking in the fire of God, in Yeshua's name, I pray.

- I decree and declare that as I bring my sacrificial offering into the courts of Heaven, the fire of God destroys any stranglehold that satan placed over my finances, in Yeshua's name.

- I decree and declare that every evil veil of darkness covering my mind and stopping my spiritual and mental transformation according to Romans 12:1 is removed in Yeshua's mighty name!

- I decree and declare that the fire of God is setting me free from every demonic mental stronghold, which has caused me to be spiritually crippled in Yeshua's name, I pray.

- I decree and declare that everything, which has been stolen from my life will now be restored back to me by the fire of God, in Yeshua's name, I pray.

## 7. End with Thanksgiving

Heavenly Father and Righteous Judge, I thank You that the foundation of Your throne is righteousness and justice. Thank You for giving me justice against the demonic entities behind these scheme of satan that is keeping me from walking in the fire of God. Heavenly Father, I thank You that because of the finished work of Yeshua on the Cross, You have translated me from the kingdom of darkness to Your glorious Kingdom of Light! Heavenly Father, since You have adopted me into Your divine family, I thank You that You always hear me, when I pray. I thank You that every apostolic and prophetic decree that I have made has been heard. Thank You, Lord, that everything I have just decreed is on its way to full manifestation in Yeshua's mighty name. Heavenly Father, until the manifestation, I will maintain an aggressive attitude of thanksgiving for the complete manifestation of what I have decreed today! In Yeshua's name I pray.

# Decrees for Commanding Your Morning

Hast thou commanded the morning since thy days; and caused the dayspring to know his place; that it might take hold of the ends of the earth, that the wicked might be shaken out of it? (**Job 38:12-13 KJV**)

## Prayer of Activation

### 1. Worship God

Heavenly Father, holy is Your name and greatly to be praised. You are the Father of Light and in You is no shadow of turning. I worship and adore You in Yeshua's name, for this purpose was I created, to give You pleasure through my love and adoration. May Your Kingdom manifest in my life as it is in Heaven. Plead my cause, O Lord, with those who strive with me; fight against any entity or person who is contending against me and what is written about me in Your book of destiny. Heavenly Father, it is written in Psalm 27:6 (NASB), *"And now my head will be lifted up above my enemies around me, and I will offer sacrifices in His tent with shouts of joy; I will sing, yes, I will sing praises to the Lord."* Heavenly Father, I thank You

that I will never be swallowed by the demonic powers because You are the Lifter of my head. Abba Father, I enjoin my worship to the heavenly chorus of worship of Your holy angels and the crowd of witnesses, in Yeshua's mighty name.

## 2. Enter the Courts of Heaven

Heavenly Father, Righteous Judge, I ask that the courts of Heaven be seated according to Daniel 7:9-10 (AMP) and that all books related to my life and destiny be opened. I ask this in Yeshua's mighty name. It is written: *"I kept looking until thrones were set up, and the Ancient of Days (God) took His seat; His garment was white as snow and the hair of His head like pure wool. His throne was flames of fire; its wheels were a burning fire. A river of fire was flowing and coming out from before Him; a thousand thousands were attending Him, and ten thousand times ten thousand were standing before Him; the court was seated, and the books were opened."* Heavenly Father, Righteous Judge, I am requesting the privilege of standing before the courtroom of the Ancient of Days according to what was revealed to the prophet Daniel, in Yeshua's name, I pray. Heavenly Father, I stand in Your royal courtroom because of the shed blood and finished work of Yeshua on the Cross. I have come to receive Your righteous judgment over my life against every evil veil that satan has been using against me. Heavenly Father, I call upon Your holy angels to be witnesses to my lawsuit and righteous prosecution of every evil entity that is working against my morning. I decree and declare that every evil veil covering my morning will be removed so I can achieve my God-given destiny here on earth, in Yeshua's name I pray.

## 3. Repent

Heavenly Father, Righteous Judge, it is written, *"If we confess our sins, He is faithful and just to forgive us our sins and to cleanse us from all unrighteousness"* (1 John 1:9 NKJV). I therefore activate the law of repentance and present

before this Court my heartfelt repentance for my personal transgressions, and for the iniquities of my forefathers that opened the door for every veil of darkness to oppress my life and bloodline, in Yeshua's name I pray. Heavenly Father, I ask that the blood of Yeshua wash away every iniquity of my forefathers that the enemy is using as a legal right to build cases against me and to bind me to every evil entity that is working against my morning. I also repent for all self-inflicted word curses and covenants with demons that have existed in my ancestral bloodline. I am asking that every ancestral agreement with demonic powers and evil altars will now be revoked. I petition the Courts of heaven to silence their right to claim me and my bloodline, in Yeshua's name. Thank You, Lord, for revoking these demonically engineered covenants and evil altars in Yeshua's mighty name! Heavenly Father and Righteous Judge, it is my heartfelt desire to divorce myself from every evil entity that is working against my morning. I petition the Ancient of Days to grant me a verdict of judicial emancipation from the oppressive power of every evil entity that is working against my morning. I receive Your favorable verdict by faith in Messiah's finished work and shed blood.

### *4. Petition the Courts of Heaven to Dismiss All of Satan's Charges*

Heavenly Father and Righteous Judge, based upon Yeshua's finished work and my heartfelt repentance, I now move on the court of Heaven to dismiss all of satan's accusations and charges against me and my bloodline in Jesus's name. Righteous Judge, dismiss every one of satan's accusation connected to every evil entity that is working against my morning. For it is written in Revelation 12:10 that the accuser of the brethren has been cast down. So, I petition You, heavenly Father and Righteous Judge, to cast down all of satan's accusations against me and dismiss all of satan's charges against me, in Yeshua's name, I pray.

## 5. Declare Your Authority in Christ

Heavenly Father and Righteous Judge, in Luke 10:19 (NKJV), Yeshua says, *"Behold, I give you the authority to trample on serpents and scorpions, and over all the power of the enemy, and nothing shall by any means hurt you."* Heavenly Father, as I prepare myself to pronounce powerful apostolic and prophetic decrees, I totally acknowledge my God-given authority in Christ to trample on serpents and scorpions that satan has weaponized against me and my destiny, in Yeshua's mighty name, I pray. The Bible also says in Proverbs 28:1 (NKJV), *"The wicked flee when no one pursues, but the righteous are bold as a lion."* Heavenly Father because of my God-given authority in Christ, I am as bold as lion. No messenger of satan, human or demonic, can intimidate me. I am like Mount Zion, which cannot be moved, in Yeshua's mighty name, I pray. I thank You, heavenly Father, that in Mark 16:17-18, Yeshua gave me the authority to cast out devils and take up serpents and to bring God's healing power to those who are sick and oppressed. I therefore make the following decrees, completely assured of both my identity and authority in Christ Jesus!

## 6. Loudly Declare These Supernatural Decrees So You Can Have Your Breakthrough:

- Heavenly Father, I decree and declare that the power of every evil entity that is working against my morning is completely broken over my life. I decree that I am no longer a victim of these demonic robbers of my morning, in Yeshua's name.

- I decree and declare that You are setting me free from every evil entity that is working against my morning in Yeshua's name.

- I decree and declare that the Holy Spirit is setting me free from any craft of witchcraft or magic that has been weaponized to destroy all the God-given potentials of my morning, in Yeshua's name, I pray.

- I decree and declare that the Holy Spirit is setting me free from every evil entity that is working against my morning that would cause me not to walk in the fullness of Kingdom assignment, in Yeshua's name, I pray.

- I decree and declare that as I bring my sacrificial offering into the courts of Heaven, the power of every evil entity that is working against my morning that satan placed over my finances is now destroyed, in Yeshua's name.

- I decree and declare that every evil entity that is working against my morning and stopping my spiritual and mental transformation according to Romans 12:1 is removed in Yeshua's mighty name!

- I decree and declare that God is setting me free from every evil entity that is working against my morning that has caused me to be spiritually crippled in Yeshua's name, I pray.

- I decree and declare that everything, which has been stolen from my life because of evil entities that are working against my morning, will now be restored back to me, in Yeshua's name, I pray.

## 7. End with Thanksgiving

Heavenly Father and Righteous Judge, I thank You that the foundation of Your throne is righteousness and justice. Thank You for giving me justice against the demonic entities that are working against my morning. Heavenly Father, I thank You that because of the finished work of Yeshua on the Cross, You have translated me from the kingdom of darkness to Your glorious Kingdom of Light! Heavenly Father, since You have adopted me into Your divine family, I thank You that You always hear me, when I pray. I thank You that every apostolic and prophetic decree that I have made has been heard. Thank You, Lord, that everything I have just decreed is on its way to full manifestation in Yeshua's mighty name. Heavenly Father, until the manifestation, I will maintain an aggressive attitude of thanksgiving for the complete manifestation of what I have decreed today! In Yeshua's name I pray.

PRAYER #32

# Decrees for Overthrowing Evil Family Altars

And behold, a man of God went from Judah to Bethel by the word of the Lord, and Jeroboam stood by the altar to burn incense. Then he cried out against the altar by the word of the Lord, and said, "O altar, altar! Thus says the Lord: 'Behold, a child, Josiah by name, shall be born to the house of David; and on you he shall sacrifice the priests of the high places who burn incense on you, and men's bones shall be burned on you.'" And he gave a sign the same day, saying, "This is the sign which the Lord has spoken: Surely the altar shall split apart, and the ashes on it shall be poured out." So it came to pass when King Jeroboam heard the saying of the man of God, who cried out against the altar in Bethel, that he stretched out his hand from the altar, saying, "Arrest him!" Then his hand, which he stretched out toward him, withered, so that he could not pull it back to himself. The altar also was split apart, and the ashes poured out from the altar, according to the sign which the man of God had given by the word of the Lord (**1 Kings 13:1-5 NKJV**).

## Prayer of Activation

### 1. Worship God

Heavenly Father, holy is Your name and greatly to be praised. You are the Father of Light and in You is no shadow of turning. I worship and adore You in Yeshua's name, for this purpose was I created, to give You pleasure through my love and adoration. May Your Kingdom manifest in my life as it is in Heaven. Plead my cause, O Lord, with those who strive with me; fight against any entity or person who is contending against me and what is written about me in Your book of destiny. Heavenly Father, it is written in Psalm 27:6 (NASB), *"And now my head will be lifted up above my enemies around me, and I will offer sacrifices in His tent with shouts of joy; I will sing, yes, I will sing praises to the Lord."* Heavenly Father, I thank You that I will never be swallowed by the demonic powers because You are the Lifter of my head. Abba Father, I enjoin my worship to the heavenly chorus of worship of Your holy angels and the crowd of witnesses, in Yeshua's mighty name.

### 2. Enter the Courts of Heaven

Heavenly Father, Righteous Judge, I ask that the courts of Heaven be seated according to Daniel 7:9-10 (AMP) and that all books related to my life and destiny be opened. I ask this in Yeshua's mighty name. It is written: *"I kept looking until thrones were set up, and the Ancient of Days (God) took His seat; His garment was white as snow and the hair of His head like pure wool. His throne was flames of fire; its wheels were a burning fire. A river of fire was flowing and coming out from before Him; a thousand thousands were attending Him, and ten thousand times ten thousand were standing before Him; the court was seated, and the books were opened."* Heavenly Father, Righteous

Judge, I am requesting the privilege of standing before the courtroom of the Ancient of Days according to what was revealed to the prophet Daniel, in Yeshua's name, I pray. Heavenly Father, I stand in Your royal courtroom because of the shed blood and finished work of Yeshua on the Cross. I have come to receive Your righteous judgment over my life against every evil family altar that satan has been using against me. Heavenly Father, I call upon Your holy angels to be witnesses to my lawsuit and righteous prosecution of every evil family altar that is working against me. I decree and declare that every evil family altar covering my spirit, soul, and body will be removed so I can achieve my God-given destiny here on earth, in Yeshua's name I pray.

## 3. Repent

Heavenly Father, Righteous Judge, it is written, *"If we confess our sins, He is faithful and just to forgive us our sins and to cleanse us from all unrighteousness"* (1 John 1:9 NKJV). I therefore activate the law of repentance and present before this court my heartfelt repentance for my personal transgressions, and for the iniquities of my forefathers that opened the door for every veil of darkness to oppress my life and bloodline, in Yeshua's name I pray. Heavenly Father, I ask that the blood of Yeshua wash away every iniquity of my forefathers that the enemy is using as a legal right to build cases against me and to bind me to every evil family altar. I also repent for all self-inflicted word curses and covenants with demons that have existed in my ancestral bloodline. I am asking that every ancestral agreement with demonic powers and evil altars will now be revoked. I petition the courts of Heaven to silence their right to claim me and my bloodline, in Yeshua's name. Thank You, Lord, for revoking these demonically engineered covenants and evil altars in Yeshua's mighty name! Heavenly Father and Righteous Judge, it is my heartfelt desire to divorce myself from every evil family altar that is operating in my life. I petition the Ancient of Days to grant me a verdict of judicial emancipation from the oppressive power of every evil family altar. I receive Your favorable verdict by faith in Messiah's finished work and shed blood.

## 4. Petition the Courts of Heaven to Dismiss All of Satan's Charges

Heavenly Father and Righteous Judge, based upon Yeshua's finished work and my heartfelt repentance, I now move on the court of Heaven to dismiss all of satan's accusations and charges against me and my bloodline in Jesus's name. Righteous Judge, dismiss every one of satan's accusation connected to every evil family altar that is oppressing my life. For it is written in Revelation 12:10 that the accuser of the brethren has been cast down. So, I petition You, heavenly Father and Righteous Judge, to cast down all of satan's accusations against me and dismiss all of satan's charges against me, in Yeshua's name, I pray.

## 5. Declare Your Authority in Christ

Heavenly Father and Righteous Judge, in Luke 10:19 (NKJV), Yeshua says, *"Behold, I give you the authority to trample on serpents and scorpions, and over all the power of the enemy, and nothing shall by any means hurt you."* Heavenly Father, as I prepare myself to pronounce powerful apostolic and prophetic decrees, I totally acknowledge my God-given authority in Christ to trample on serpents and scorpions that satan has weaponized against me and my destiny, in Yeshua's mighty name, I pray. The Bible also says in Proverbs 28:1 (NKJV), *"The wicked flee when no one pursues, but the righteous are bold as a lion."* Heavenly Father, because of my God-given authority in Christ, I am as bold as lion. No messenger of satan, human or demonic, can intimidate me. I am like Mount Zion, which cannot be moved, in Yeshua's mighty name, I pray. I thank You, heavenly Father, that in Mark 16:17-18, Yeshua gave me the authority to cast out devils and take up serpents and to bring God's healing power to those who are sick and oppressed. I therefore make the following decrees, completely assured of both my identity and authority in Christ Jesus!

## *6. Loudly Declare These Supernatural Decrees So You Can Have Your Breakthrough:*

- Heavenly Father, I decree and declare that the power of every evil family altar of darkness is completely broken over my life. I decree that I am no longer a victim of these demonic family altars, in Yeshua's name.

- I decree and declare that You are setting me free from every evil family altar that causes physical and spiritual deafness in Yeshua's name.

- I decree and declare that the Holy Spirit is setting me free from any evil family altar of witchcraft or magic that has caused any kind of spiritual blindness in my life, in Yeshua's name, I pray.

- I decree and declare that the Holy Spirit is setting me free from every evil family altar of deception that would cause me not to walk in the truthfulness of God's Word, in Yeshua's name, I pray.

- I decree and declare that as I bring my sacrificial offering into the courts of Heaven, the power of every evil family altar that satan placed over my finances is now destroyed, in Yeshua's name.

- I decree and declare that every evil family altar covering my mind and stopping my spiritual and mental transformation according to Romans 12:1 is removed in Yeshua's mighty name!

- I decree and declare that God is setting me free from every evil family altar, which has caused me to be spiritually crippled in Yeshua's name, I pray.

- I decree and declare that everything, which has been stolen from my life because of evil family altars, will now be restored back to me, in Yeshua's name, I pray.

## 7. End with Thanksgiving

Heavenly Father and Righteous Judge, I thank You that the foundation of Your throne is righteousness and justice. Thank You for giving me justice against the demonic entities behind these evil family altars. Heavenly Father, I thank You that because of the finished work of Yeshua on the Cross, You have translated me from the kingdom of darkness to Your glorious Kingdom of Light! Heavenly Father, since You have adopted me into Your divine family, I thank You that You always hear me, when I pray. I thank You that every apostolic and prophetic decree that I have made has been heard. Thank You, Lord, that everything I have just decreed is on its way to full manifestation in Yeshua's mighty name. Heavenly Father, until the manifestation, I will maintain an aggressive attitude of thanksgiving for the complete manifestation of what I have decreed today! In Yeshua's name I pray.

# Decrees for Releasing Divine Protection

He who dwells in the secret place of the Most High shall abide under the shadow of the Almighty. I will say of the Lord, "He is my refuge and my fortress; my God, in Him I will trust." Surely He shall deliver you from the snare of the fowler and from the perilous pestilence. He shall cover you with His feathers, and under His wings you shall take refuge; His truth shall be your shield and buckler. You shall not be afraid of the terror by night, nor of the arrow that flies by day (**Psalm 91:1-5 NKJV**).

## Prayer of Activation

### *1. Worship God*

Heavenly Father, holy is Your name and greatly to be praised. You are the Father of Light and in You is no shadow of turning. I worship and adore You in Yeshua's name, for this purpose was I created, to give You pleasure through my love and adoration. May Your Kingdom manifest in my life as it is in Heaven. Plead my cause, O Lord, with those who strive with me; fight against any entity or person who is contending against me and what is written about me in Your book of destiny. Heavenly Father, it is written in Psalm 27:6 (NASB), *"And now my head will be lifted up above*

*my enemies around me, and I will offer sacrifices in His tent with shouts of joy; I will sing, yes, I will sing praises to the Lord."* Heavenly Father, I thank You that I will never be swallowed by the demonic powers because You are the Lifter of my head. Abba Father, I enjoin my worship to the heavenly chorus of worship of Your holy angels and the crowd of witnesses, in Yeshua's mighty name.

## 2. Enter the Courts of Heaven

Heavenly Father, Righteous Judge, I ask that the Courts of Heaven be seated according to Daniel 7:9-10 (AMP) and that all books related to my life and destiny be opened. I ask this in Yeshua's mighty name. It is written: *"I kept looking until thrones were set up, and the Ancient of Days (God) took His seat; His garment was white as snow and the hair of His head like pure wool. His throne was flames of fire; its wheels were a burning fire. A river of fire was flowing and coming out from before Him; a thousand thousands were attending Him, and ten thousand times ten thousand were standing before Him; the court was seated, and the books were opened."* Heavenly Father, Righteous Judge, I am requesting the privilege of standing before the courtroom of the Ancient of Days according to what was revealed to the prophet Daniel, in Yeshua's name, I pray. Heavenly Father, I stand in Your royal courtroom because of the shed blood and finished work of Yeshua on the Cross. I have come to receive Your righteous judgment over my life concerning my divine protection from every evil scheme of satan. Heavenly Father, I call upon Your holy angels to be witnesses to my lawsuit and righteous prosecution of every evil scheme of satan that is working against my divine protection. I decree and declare that I am divinely protected in my spirit, soul, and body so I can achieve my God-given destiny here on earth, in Yeshua's name I pray.

## 3. Repent

Heavenly Father, Righteous Judge, it is written, *"If we confess our sins, He is faithful and just to forgive us our sins and to cleanse us from all unrighteousness"* (1 John 1:9 NKJV). I therefore activate the law of repentance and present before this court my heartfelt repentance for my personal transgressions, and for the iniquities of my forefathers that opened the door for every veil of darkness to oppress my life and bloodline, in Yeshua's name I pray. Heavenly Father, I ask that the blood of Yeshua wash away every iniquity of my forefathers that the enemy is using as a legal right to build cases against me and to rob me of my divine protection. I also repent for all self-inflicted word curses and covenants with demons that have existed in my ancestral bloodline. I am asking that every ancestral agreement with demonic powers and evil altars will now be revoked. I petition the courts of Heaven to silence their right to claim me and my bloodline, in Yeshua's name. Thank You, Lord, for revoking these demonically engineered covenants and evil altars in Yeshua's mighty name! Heavenly Father and Righteous Judge, it is my heartfelt desire to divorce myself from every work of darkness that can compromise my divine protection. I petition the Ancient of Days to grant me a verdict of judicial emancipation and protection from the oppressive power of spirits of darkness. I receive Your favorable verdict by faith in Messiah's finished work and shed blood.

## 4. Petition the Courts of Heaven to Dismiss All of Satan's Charges

Heavenly Father and Righteous Judge, based upon Yeshua's finished work and my heartfelt repentance, I now move on the court of Heaven to dismiss all of satan's accusations and charges against me and my bloodline in Jesus's name. Righteous Judge, dismiss every one of satan's accusation connected to every evil spirit that is contending against my divine protection. For it is written in Revelation 12:10 that the accuser of the brethren has been cast down. So, I petition You, heavenly Father and Righteous Judge, to cast down all of satan's accusations against me and dismiss all of satan's charges against me, in Yeshua's name, I pray.

## 5. Declare Your Authority in Christ

Heavenly Father and Righteous Judge, in Luke 10:19 (NKJV), Yeshua says, *"Behold, I give you the authority to trample on serpents and scorpions, and over all the power of the enemy, and nothing shall by any means hurt you."* Heavenly Father, as I prepare myself to pronounce powerful apostolic and prophetic decrees, I totally acknowledge my God-given authority in Christ to trample on serpents and scorpions that satan has weaponized against me and my destiny, in Yeshua's mighty name, I pray. The Bible also says in Proverbs 28:1 (NKJV), *"The wicked flee when no one pursues, but the righteous are bold as a lion."* Heavenly Father, because of my God-given authority in Christ, I am as bold as lion. No messenger of satan, human or demonic, can intimidate me. I am like Mount Zion, which cannot be moved, in Yeshua's mighty name, I pray. I thank You, heavenly Father, that in Mark 16:17-18, Yeshua gave me the authority to cast out devils and take up serpents and to bring God's healing power to those who are sick and oppressed. I therefore make the following decrees, completely assured of both my identity and authority in Christ Jesus!

## 6. Loudly Declare These Supernatural Decrees So You Can Have Your Breakthrough:

- Heavenly Father, I decree and declare my divine protection from the power of every spirit of darkness. I decree that I am no longer a victim of these demonic umbrellas of darkness, in Yeshua's name.

- I decree and declare that You are setting me free from every evil spirit that causes physical and spiritual deafness in Yeshua's name.

- I decree and declare that the Holy Spirit is setting me free from any spirit of witchcraft or magic that has caused any kind of spiritual blindness in my life, in Yeshua's name, I pray.

- I decree and declare that the Holy Spirit is setting me free from every veil of deception that would cause me not to walk in the truthfulness of God's Word, in Yeshua's name, I pray.

- I decree and declare that as I bring my sacrificial offering into the courts of Heaven, the power of every evil spirit that satan placed over my finances is now destroyed, in Yeshua's name.

- I decree and declare that every evil veil of darkness covering my mind and stopping my spiritual and mental transformation according to Romans 12:1 is removed in Yeshua's mighty name!

- I decree and declare that God is setting me free from every demonic technology, which has caused me to be spiritually crippled in Yeshua's name, I pray.

- I decree and declare that everything, which has been stolen from my life because of the power of darkness, will now be restored back to me, in Yeshua's name, I pray.

## 7. End with Thanksgiving

Heavenly Father and Righteous Judge, I thank You that the foundation of Your throne is righteousness and justice. Thank You for giving me justice and divine protection against the demonic entities behind all the works of darkness. Heavenly Father, I thank You that because of the finished work of Yeshua on the Cross, You have translated me from the kingdom of darkness to Your glorious Kingdom of Light! Heavenly Father, since You have adopted me into Your divine family, I thank You that You always hear me, when I pray. I thank You that every apostolic and prophetic decree that I have made has been heard. Thank You, Lord, that everything I have just decreed is on its way to full manifestation in Yeshua's mighty name. Heavenly Father, until the manifestation, I will maintain an aggressive attitude of thanksgiving for the complete manifestation of what I have decreed today! In Yeshua's name I pray.

# Decrees for Overriding Evil Man-Made Protocols

Now it happened on the third day that Esther put on her royal robes and stood in the inner court of the king's palace, across from the king's house, while the king sat on his royal throne in the royal house, facing the entrance of the house. So it was, when the king saw Queen Esther standing in the court, that she found favor in his sight, and the king held out to Esther the golden scepter that was in his hand. Then Esther went near and touched the top of the scepter. And the king said to her, "What do you wish, Queen Esther? What is your request? It shall be given to you—up to half the kingdom!" So Esther answered, "If it pleases the king, let the king and Haman come today to the banquet that I have prepared for him." Then the king said, "Bring Haman quickly, that he may do as Esther has said." So the king and Haman went to the banquet that Esther had prepared. At the banquet of wine the king said to Esther, "What is your petition? It shall be granted you. What is your request, up to half the kingdom? It shall be done!" Then Esther answered and said, "My petition and request is this: If I have found favor in the sight of the king, and if it pleases the king to grant my petition and fulfill my request, then let the king and Haman come to the banquet which I will prepare for them, and tomorrow I will do as the king has said." So Haman went out that day joyful and with a glad heart; but when Haman saw Mordecai in the king's gate, and that he did not stand or tremble before him, he was filled with indignation against Mordecai (**Esther 5:1-9 NKJV**).

## Prayer of Activation

### 1. Worship God

Heavenly Father, holy is Your name and greatly to be praised. You are the Father of Light and in You is no shadow of turning. I worship and adore You in Yeshua's name, for this purpose was I created, to give You pleasure through my love and adoration. May Your Kingdom manifest in my life as it is in Heaven. Plead my cause, O Lord, with those who strive with me; fight against any entity or person who is contending against me and what is written about me in Your book of destiny. Heavenly Father, it is written in Psalm 27:6 (NASB), *"And now my head will be lifted up above my enemies around me, and I will offer sacrifices in His tent with shouts of joy; I will sing, yes, I will sing praises to the Lord."* Heavenly Father, I thank You that I will never be swallowed by the demonic powers because You are the Lifter of my head. Abba Father, I enjoin my worship to the heavenly chorus of worship of Your holy angels and the crowd of witnesses, in Yeshua's mighty name.

### 2. Enter the Courts of Heaven

Heavenly Father, Righteous Judge, I ask that the courts of Heaven be seated according to Daniel 7:9-10 (AMP) and that all books related to my life and destiny be opened. I ask this in Yeshua's mighty name. It is written: *"I kept looking until thrones were set up, and the Ancient of Days (God) took His seat; His garment was white as snow and the hair of His head like pure wool. His throne was flames of fire; its wheels were a burning fire. A river of fire was flowing and coming out from before Him; a thousand thousands were attending Him, and ten thousand times ten thousand were standing before Him; the court was seated, and the books were opened."* Heavenly Father, Righteous

Judge, I am requesting the privilege of standing before the courtroom of the Ancient of Days according to what was revealed to the prophet Daniel, in Yeshua's name, I pray. Heavenly Father, I stand in Your royal courtroom because of the shed blood and finished work of Yeshua on the Cross. I have come to receive Your righteous judgment over my life against every evil and man-made protocol that satan has been using against me. Heavenly Father, I call upon Your holy angels to be witnesses to my lawsuit and righteous prosecution of every evil and man-made protocol that is working against me. I decree and declare that every evil and man-made protocol that is blocking my destiny will be removed so I can move forward, in Yeshua's name I pray.

## 3. Repent

Heavenly Father, Righteous Judge, it is written, *"If we confess our sins, He is faithful and just to forgive us our sins and to cleanse us from all unrighteousness"* (1 John 1:9 NKJV). I therefore activate the law of repentance and present before this court my heartfelt repentance for my personal transgressions, and for the iniquities of my forefathers that opened the door for every veil of darkness to oppress my life and bloodline, in Yeshua's name I pray. Heavenly Father, I ask that the blood of Yeshua wash away every iniquity of my forefathers that the enemy is using as a legal right to build cases against me and to bind me to every evil and man-made protocol. I also repent for all self-inflicted word curses and covenants with demons that have existed in my ancestral bloodline. I am asking that every ancestral agreement with demonic powers and evil altars will now be revoked. I petition the courts of heaven to silence their right to claim me and my bloodline, in Yeshua's name. Thank You, Lord, for revoking these demonically engineered covenants and evil altars in Yeshua's mighty name! Heavenly Father and Righteous Judge, it is my heartfelt desire to divorce myself from every evil and man-made protocol that is operating in my life. I petition the Ancient of Days to grant me a verdict of judicial emancipation from the oppressive power of every evil and man-made protocol. I receive Your favorable verdict by faith in Messiah's finished work and shed blood.

## 4. Petition the Courts of Heaven to Dismiss All of Satan's Charges

Heavenly Father and Righteous Judge, based upon Yeshua's finished work and my heartfelt repentance, I now move on the Court of Heaven to dismiss all of satan's accusations and charges against me and my bloodline in Jesus's name. Righteous Judge, dismiss every one of satan's accusation connected to every evil and man-made protocol that is oppressing my life. For it is written in Revelation 12:10 that the accuser of the brethren has been cast down. So, I petition You, heavenly Father and Righteous Judge, to cast down all of satan's accusations against me and dismiss all of satan's charges against me, in Yeshua's name, I pray.

## 5. Declare Your Authority in Christ

Heavenly Father and Righteous Judge, in Luke 10:19 (NKJV), Yeshua says, *"Behold, I give you the authority to trample on serpents and scorpions, and over all the power of the enemy, and nothing shall by any means hurt you."* Heavenly Father as I prepare myself to pronounce powerful apostolic and prophetic decrees, I totally acknowledge my God-given authority in Christ to trample on serpents and scorpions that satan has weaponized against me and my destiny, in Yeshua's mighty name, I pray. The Bible also says in Proverbs 28:1 (NKJV), *"The wicked flee when no one pursues, but the righteous are bold as a lion."* Heavenly Father because of my God-given authority in Christ, I am as bold as lion. No messenger of satan, human or demonic, can intimidate me. I am like Mount Zion, which cannot be moved, in Yeshua's mighty name, I pray. I thank You, heavenly Father, that in Mark 16:17-18, Yeshua gave me the authority to cast out devils and take up serpents and to bring God's healing power to those who are sick and oppressed. I therefore make the following decrees, completely assured of both my identity and authority in Christ Jesus!

## 6. Loudly Declare These Supernatural Decrees So You Can Have Your Breakthrough:

- Heavenly Father, I decree and declare that the power of every evil and man-made protocol is completely broken over my life. I decree that I am no longer a victim of these evil and manmade protocols, in Yeshua's name.

- I decree and declare that You are setting me free from every evil and man-made protocol that causes delays in destiny, in Yeshua's name.

- I decree and declare that the Holy Spirit is setting me free from any evil and man-made protocol that has caused any kind of spiritual blindness in my life, in Yeshua's name, I pray.

- I decree and declare that the Holy Spirit is setting me free from every evil and man-made protocol that would cause me not to walk in the truthfulness of God's Word, in Yeshua's name, I pray.

- I decree and declare that as I bring my sacrificial offering into the courts of Heaven, the power of every evil and man-made protocol that satan placed over my finances is now destroyed, in Yeshua's name.

- I decree and declare that every evil and man-made protocol stopping my spiritual and mental transformation according to Romans 12:1 is removed in Yeshua's mighty name!

- I decree and declare that God is setting me free from every evil and man-made protocol, which has caused me to be spiritually crippled in Yeshua's name, I pray.

- I decree and declare that everything, which has been stolen from my life because of evil and man-made protocols, will now be restored back to me, in Yeshua's name, I pray.

## 7. End with Thanksgiving

Heavenly Father and Righteous Judge, I thank You that the foundation of Your throne is righteousness and justice. Thank You for giving me justice against the demonic entities behind these evil and man-made protocols. Heavenly Father, I thank You that because of the finished work of Yeshua on the Cross, You have translated me from the kingdom of darkness to Your glorious Kingdom of Light! Heavenly Father, since You have adopted me into Your divine family, I thank You that You always hear me, when I pray. I thank You that every apostolic and prophetic decree that I have made has been heard. Thank You, Lord, that everything I have just decreed is on its way to full manifestation in Yeshua's mighty name. Heavenly Father, until the manifestation, I will maintain an aggressive attitude of thanksgiving for the complete manifestation of what I have decreed today! In Yeshua's name I pray.

# About Dr. Francis Myles

Dr. Francis Myles is a multi-gifted international motivational speaker, business consultant, and apostle to the nations. He is the senior pastor of Dream Genesis Church International in Lusaka, Zambia. He is also the creator and founder of the world's first Marketplace Bible and founder of Francis Myles International, a TV and multimedia ministry based in Atlanta, Georgia, USA.

Dr. Myles is a sought-after conference speaker in both ministerial and marketplace seminars. He is also a spiritual life coach to "movers and shakers" in the marketplace and political arena. He has appeared on TBN, GodTV, and Daystar, and has been a featured guest on Sid Roth's *It's Supernatural!* TV show and "This Is Your Day" with Pastor Benny Hinn.

Dr. Myles is happily married to the love of his life, Carmela Real Myles, and they reside in McDonough, a suburb of Atlanta, Georgia.